CAMPAIGNS IN MISSISSIPPI AND TENNESSEE

FEBRUARY–DECEMBER 1864

by
Derek W. Frisby

Center of Military History
United States Army
Washington, D.C., 2014

Introduction

Although over one hundred fifty years have passed since the start of the American Civil War, that titanic conflict continues to matter. The forces unleashed by that war were immensely destructive because of the significant issues involved: the existence of the Union, the end of slavery, and the very future of the nation. The war remains our most contentious, and our bloodiest, with over six hundred thousand killed in the course of the four-year struggle.

Most civil wars do not spring up overnight, and the American Civil War was no exception. The seeds of the conflict were sown in the earliest days of the republic's founding, primarily over the existence of slavery and the slave trade. Although no conflict can begin without the conscious decisions of those engaged in the debates at that moment, in the end, there was simply no way to paper over the division of the country into two camps: one that was dominated by slavery and the other that sought first to limit its spread and then to abolish it. Our nation was indeed "half slave and half free," and that could not stand.

Regardless of the factors tearing the nation asunder, the soldiers on each side of the struggle went to war for personal reasons: looking for adventure, being caught up in the passions and emotions of their peers, believing in the Union, favoring states' rights, or even justifying the simple schoolyard dynamic of being convinced that they were "worth" three of the soldiers on the other side. Nor can we overlook the factor that some went to war to prove their manhood. This has been, and continues to be, a key dynamic in understanding combat and the profession of arms. Soldiers join for many reasons but often stay in the fight because of their comrades and because they do not want to seem like cowards. Sometimes issues of national impact shrink to nothing in the intensely personal world of cannon shell and minié ball.

Whatever the reasons, the struggle was long and costly and only culminated with the conquest of the rebellious Confederacy, the preservation of the Union, and the end of slavery. These campaign pamphlets on the American Civil War, prepared in commemoration of our national sacrifices, seek to remember that war and honor those in the United States Army who died to preserve the Union and free the slaves as well as to tell the story of those American soldiers who fought for the Confederacy despite the inherently flawed nature of their cause. The Civil War was our greatest struggle and continues to deserve our deep study and contemplation.

RICHARD W. STEWART
Chief Historian

Campaigns in Mississippi and Tennessee
February–December 1864

Strategic Setting

As 1863 gave way to 1864, the American Civil War concluded its pivotal year. In the East, the Confederates' long-odds victory at Chancellorsville, Virginia, in May was trumped by the Union triumph at Gettysburg, Pennsylvania, two months later. In Mississippi, the eight-month Vicksburg Campaign culminated in the surrender of the Confederate garrison on the Fourth of July and the opening of the Mississippi River. In Tennessee, Union victories at Knoxville and Chattanooga in November negated the Confederates' stunning success at Chickamauga, Georgia, two months earlier.

Having secured Chattanooga—the "Gateway to the Deep South"—as a forward base, three Union armies were preparing for a spring campaign to capture Atlanta, Georgia: the Army of the Tennessee commanded by Maj. Gen. William T. Sherman, the Army of the Cumberland led by Maj. Gen. George H. Thomas, and the XI Corps and XII Corps from the Army of the Potomac under Maj. Gen. Joseph Hooker. A fourth Federal army, the Army of the Ohio led by Maj. Gen. Ambrose E. Burnside, held Knoxville and thus blocked the Confederate railroad linking Virginia with Tennessee. The overall commander of these four armies was Maj. Gen. Ulysses S. Grant, whose geographic command, the Military Division of the Mississippi, encompassed most of the

Western Theater as well as the Department of Arkansas in the Trans-Mississippi region. As the Union Army's most successful commander, Grant had overseen the operations that captured Vicksburg and that routed the Confederate Army of Tennessee at Chattanooga.

After being driven from the mountain ridges overlooking the Gateway City, the Army of Tennessee withdrew into northwestern Georgia to rest and refit for the spring campaign season. On 1 December, the army's much-maligned commander, General Braxton Bragg, tendered his resignation, and one month later, Confederate President Jefferson Davis replaced him with the far more popular—and far more cautious—General Joseph E. Johnston. Having failed to capture Knoxville, the Confederate expeditionary force under Lt. Gen. James Longstreet spent the winter of 1864 in eastern Tennessee to prevent the Army of the Ohio from reinforcing Grant at Chattanooga before returning to the Army of Northern Virginia in the spring.

As the third year of the war drew to a close, the Confederate Congress took steps to fill the rebel army's thinning ranks. In December 1863, the Southern legislature abolished the law permitting conscripts to hire substitutes, and in February 1864, it lowered the minimum draft age from eighteen to seventeen and raised the maximum age from forty-five to fifty. The new law also extended three-year enlistments—many of them about to expire—to the end of the war. But when President Davis received a proposal from the Army of Tennessee to recruit and arm slaves, he immediately suppressed the document, deeming its implications too revolutionary to consider.

The Federal government also sought to replenish the Union Army's shrinking frontline troop strength siphoned off by occupation duty, combat casualties, sickness, and desertion. Fortunately for the Federals, the North had a much larger manpower pool to draw from than did the South, which meant that the U.S. Congress did not have to resort to expanding draft age limits or extending service terms. To attract enlistees, local, state, and Federal agencies offered cash bounties, a practice that achieved some success, but at the cost of rampant corruption. As the Union Army occupied more and more Southern territory, a new source of recruits materialized in the form of white Unionists and former slaves, with the latter enlisting in the U.S. Colored Troops (USCT). By the end of the war, roughly 120,000 white Southern loyalists and 180,000 black soldiers had served in the Union Army.

The Federal army's gravest concern in early 1864 was the imminent departure of tens of thousands of veteran troops due to the expiration of their three-year enlistments. In an effort to retain as many of these "Heroes of Sixty-One" as possible, Congress authorized several incentives, including cash bonuses, furloughs, and special unit insignias denoting the soldiers' "veteranized" status. Roughly one-half of these men reenlisted, and yet the departure of the remainder—combined with the furloughs of the reenlisting veterans—would disrupt the Union Army's campaign for the spring of 1864.

In January 1864, the immediate challenge for Union commanders in Mississippi and Tennessee lay in suppressing the Confederate cavalry raiders, local partisan units, and rogue bands of guerrillas and bushwhackers who infested the rear areas and preyed on the Federals' vulnerable lines of communications. Union generals deployed numerous troop detachments to guard railroads and bridges and to repair them when they were damaged, thereby reducing the army's offensive capability and leaving the detachments isolated and exposed to attack. Worse yet, roughly thirty thousand recently paroled Confederates from Vicksburg had just been turned loose on the countryside, leading General Sherman to fear that they would augment the irregular forces already in the region and disrupt preparations for the spring campaign in Georgia.

General Sherman
(Library of Congress)

By January 1864, Sherman ranked as one of the Union Army's most resourceful generals when it came to dealing with guerrillas and bushwhackers. At first, he tried to distinguish between law-abiding civilians and those who actively aided enemy combatants. But he soon abandoned that policy when it became apparent that the Confederates made no such distinction in their treatment of Southern Unionists. Even so, Sherman hesitated to retaliate out of respect for the laws of war until he came to the realization that he was fighting not merely the Confederate Army but the Southern people as well. "The Army of the Confederacy is the South," he asserted. "The entire South, man, woman, and child, are against us, armed and determined." He thus came to the conclusion that the only remedy for the guerrilla problem was to hold the citizenry fully accountable and to treat them as accessories. During his tenure as military governor of Memphis, Tennessee, Sherman had retaliated against bushwhackers firing on the Union supply ship *Eugene* by burning the town where the shots had originated, and had threatened to banish ten families from Memphis for each additional vessel that was fired on. Since then, his thinking had evolved from targeted retaliation against known enemies into a "hard war" concept that sanctioned large-scale destruction to disrupt the Confederacy's war-making capability and damage its morale.

Operations

The Meridian Campaign

Sherman returned from a Christmas visit to his family with a renewed determination to wreak havoc on the Confederacy and with an audacious plan for doing just that. For several months, he had contemplated a raid on Meridian, Mississippi, a Confederate supply center and the junction of three important railroads: the Mobile and Ohio, the Southern Railroad of Mississippi, and the Alabama and Mississippi Rivers Railroad. Instead of waiting for springtime weather, he proposed a surprise midwinter offensive launched from Vicksburg and Memphis, striking the key rail hub and—if feasible—pushing on to Selma, Alabama. The main objective of his raid was to destroy railroads, stores, industries, and anything else along his route that could support the Confederacy. The resulting destruction, he reasoned, would hinder the Confederate Army's ability to threaten Vicksburg or to defend Atlanta in the upcoming campaign. To maintain the initiative, Sherman would have to move quickly and strike hard. From his experience in the Vicksburg Campaign, the general knew that his men could travel light and live off the land.

In presenting his plan to Grant, Sherman argued that the Meridian raid would eliminate Mississippi as a Confederate supply base for months, thus freeing thousands of Union troops for the Atlanta Campaign who might otherwise be tied down on occupation duty. Grant authorized Sherman's raid but cautioned him to end it by early March in order to support Maj. Gen. Nathaniel P. Banks' Red River expedition in the Trans-Mississippi.

Sherman accordingly issued orders to the commanders of the two infantry corps who would participate in the raid: XVI Corps commander Maj. Gen. Stephen A. Hurlbut at Memphis and XVII Corps commander Maj. Gen. James B. McPherson at Vicksburg. Each general was to assemble a two-division force totaling about ten thousand men and depart from Vicksburg by the start of February 1864. On 27 January, Hurlbut boarded his troops on transports and sent them down the Mississippi River to Vicksburg, where they arrived on 1 February. Sherman's force comprised about twenty-five thousand men, including infantry, artillery, and a cavalry battalion that would screen the advance. Hurlbut's column would march on a route that ran a few miles north of McPherson's route until they reached Jackson, the Mississippi state capital, where the two columns would converge.

Sherman directed that the left flank of his force be screened by a 7,000-man cavalry column led by Brig. Gen. William Sooy Smith. Smith was slated to depart from Memphis on 1 February; his orders were to prevent Maj. Gen. Nathan Bedford Forrest's Confederate cavalry from interfering with the Meridian raid and to rendezvous with Sherman at Meridian by 10 February. In addition, Sherman requested that Grant send a joint Army-Navy force up the Yazoo River north of Vicksburg to threaten the rail hub at Grenada, Mississippi. He also asked that Thomas feint on Johnston in northern Georgia and that Banks—whose headquarters was at New Orleans, Louisiana—launch diversionary maneuvers by land and sea toward Mobile, Alabama. He hoped that these demonstrations would prevent the Confederates from reinforcing Lt. Gen. Leonidas Polk's command in Mississippi and thereby enable the Federals to enter Meridian virtually unopposed.

Sherman regarded his raid as a gamble, but he maintained that "we must in war risk a good deal." There would be no line of communications stretching back to Vicksburg: should the enemy concentrate against him, Sherman could expect no reinforcements aside from Smith's cavalry column. And he was under pressure to finish the raid in time to support Banks' Red River expedition.

On 3 February, the two Federal columns, with Hurlbut's XVI Corps on the left and McPherson's XVII Corps on the right, set out from the "Gibraltar of the West," and began the 150-mile march to Meridian. Officers and men alike traveled without tents or personal baggage, but at the outset they were favored by unseasonably mild weather. The wagons carried only ammunition and some hardtack and coffee; foraging details would have to supply the rest. Lacking commu-

General Polk
(Valentine Richmond History Center)

nications with Smith's cavalry force, Sherman would remain unaware of developments on his left flank until contact could be reestablished near Meridian. Sherman was confident that Smith's force heavily outnumbered Forrest's, but he also believed that the Confederate cavalry was more experienced and that it was led by one of the war's most brilliant cavalry officers. In any event, Sherman relied on speed and superior striking power to overcome any obstacle that might present itself (*Map 1*).

The two infantry columns crossed the Big Black River about ten miles east of Vicksburg, heading toward Jackson. Sherman traveled with the XVI Corps because he lacked confidence in Hurlbut and wanted to be with the column that was closer to Forrest's cavalry. As the Federals passed through the site of the May 1863 Battle of Champion Hill, a small force of Confederate cavalry and artillery made a brief stand against McPherson's advance. Hurlbut also encountered light resistance just to the north, but both Union columns quickly swept aside the Southern defenders, sustaining minimal casualties. On 6 February, Sherman entered Jackson, his advance driving a detachment of Confederate cavalry through the streets of the town and out the other side. He was

ADVANCE ON MERIDIAN
3 February–3 March 1864
Union Advance
Battle
0   25   50
Miles
TENNESSEE
ARKANSAS
MISSISSIPPI
ALABAMA
Huntingdon
Fort Pillow
Jackson
Randolph
Bolivar
Memphis
11 Feb
26 Feb
Colliersville
Corinth
Hernando
Holly Springs
SMITH
Ripley
Tunica
Helena
New Albany
SMITH
Oxford
Pontotoc
Tupelo
IVEY FARM
22 Feb
18 Feb
Okolona
OKOLONA
22 Feb
Aberdeen
Grenada
20 Feb
WEST POINT
20–21 Feb
Columbus
Greenwood
Greenville
MISSISSIPPI
Macon
Richland
Yazoo City
Carthage
Canton
SHERMAN
SHERMAN
Union
Vicksburg
3 Mar
Hillsboro
Decatur
20 Feb
3 Feb
6 Feb
Morton
Brandon
14 Feb
JACKSON
SHERMAN
Meridian
Southern RR
to Selma
Alabama and Mississippi Rivers RR
Memphis and Ohio RR
Tennessee and Ohio RR
Memphis and Charleston RR
Tennessee R
Mississippi and Tennessee RR
Mississippi Central RR
Mobile and Ohio RR
Mississippi Central RR
Mobile and Ohio RR
Mississippi R
Yazoo R
Big Black R
Pearl R

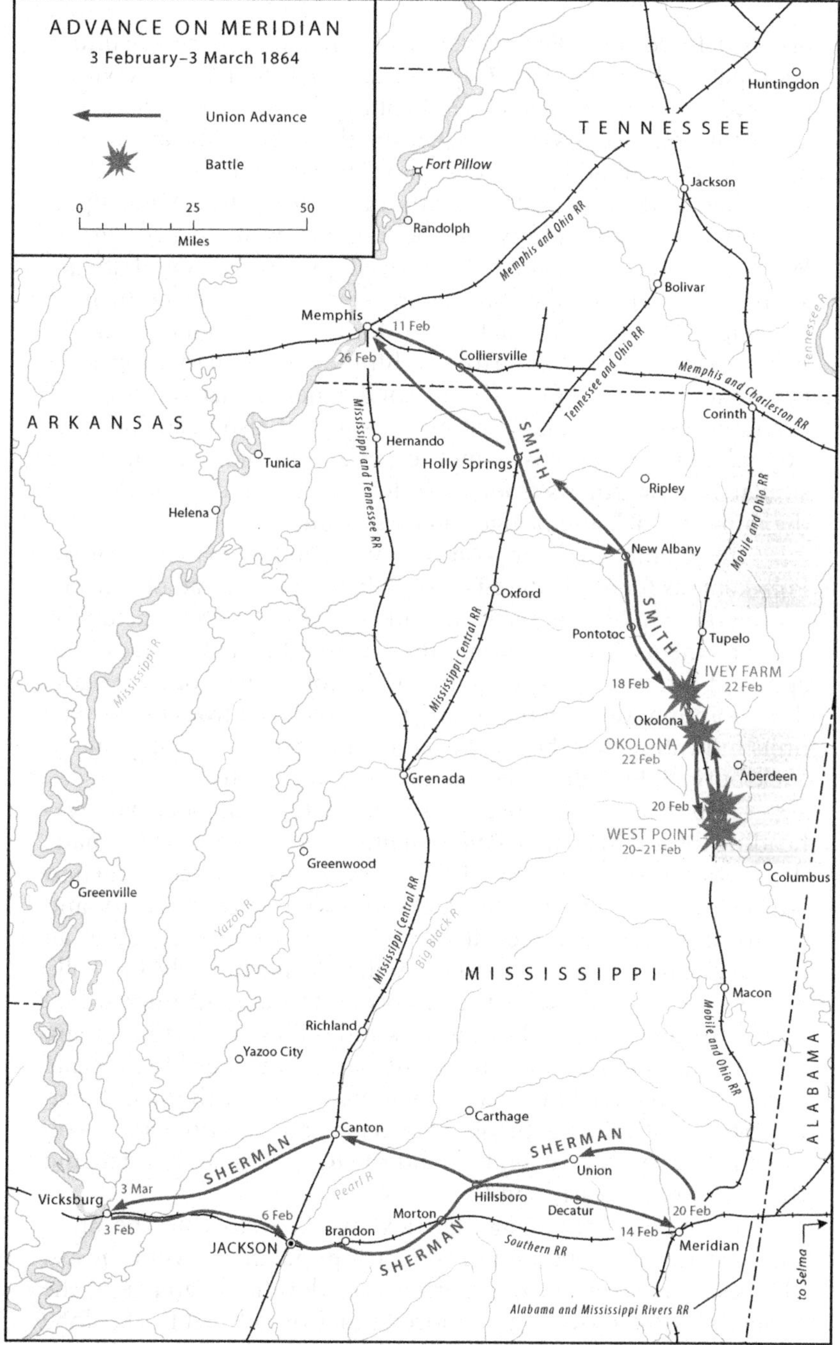

MAP 1

briefly delayed at the Pearl River, while the Pioneer Brigade under his capable chief engineer, Capt. Andrew Hickenlooper, repaired the bridge there. The two Federal columns were soon across, and Sherman breathed a sigh of relief, for the last significant natural obstacle on the road to Meridian now lay behind him.

Sherman's force cut a swath through central Mississippi, enjoying the rich bounty of the region's well-stocked farms. Whatever property that had survived previous Federal incursions was either looted or burned by Sherman's men, who seemed to delight in their destructive work. They nicknamed Jackson "Chimneyville" because the town's chimneys were all that appeared to remain standing. One Union soldier noted that the town of Brandon just a few miles east of Jackson had also been "purified by fire." Many other Mississippi towns and plantations suffered a similar fate. Sherman's troops also found time to destroy most of the railroad track and bridges on their route.

The Confederate opposition, meanwhile, was in disarray. Polk kept his forces scattered across Mississippi instead of concentrating them in Sherman's front, and he pleaded with Johnston for reinforcements. But Johnston refused to send them because of the apparent threat to his own command in northern Georgia. No less disappointing were the reports that Polk received from his cavalry units indicating that they had tried to cut Sherman's supply line to Vicksburg, only to discover that no such line existed.

Despite the insistence of subordinates that Sherman was heading toward Meridian, Polk remained convinced that Sherman's destination was Mobile. By 11 February, as Sherman continued to advance due east well beyond Jackson, Polk realized his error and began to gather his forces at Meridian for use in evacuating all military supplies to Demopolis, Alabama. Fortunately for Polk, Maj. George Whitfield of the Confederate Railroad Bureau had already begun to collect locomotives and rolling stock at Meridian. Working around the clock, the Confederates managed to evacuate everything that could be loaded onto train cars, with the last load departing just minutes before Sherman's arrival on the afternoon of 14 February. The Federals found the town almost deserted and the warehouses nearly empty.

Sherman's force spent the next week destroying the area's war-sustaining resources and the local population's will to resist. The result was staggering. During the Meridian Campaign, the Federals wrecked over one hundred miles of railroad track, along with numerous bridges and other structures, nineteen locomotives, twenty-eight rail cars, and untold amounts of equipment and supplies. Sherman boasted that "Meridian, with its depots, storehouses, arsenal, hospitals, offices, hotels, and cantonments no longer exists." In the meantime, he anxiously awaited the arrival of Smith's cavalry before moving on to Selma. But Smith had drawn Forrest's full attention and was now engaged in a desperate struggle for survival one hundred miles north of Meridian.

W. S. Smith's mounted column had to cover 250 miles through hostile territory, much of it controlled by Forrest's cavalry. Sherman had reluctantly agreed to let Smith command the detachment in deference to Grant, but he remained dubious of the Ohioan's abilities. He therefore designated Brig. Gen. Benjamin H. Grierson as Smith's second in command. An excellent cavalry officer, Grierson had chased Forrest the previous December until a blizzard put an abrupt end to his pursuit on New Year's Eve 1863. Perhaps most importantly, Grierson knew the country they would be passing through.

General W. S. Smith
(Massachusetts MOLLUS Collection
U.S. Army Military History Institute)

At least Smith was nothing if not industrious. Within the brief span of time allotted to him, he had transferred his cavalry units from middle Tennessee to Memphis, and had collected every available horse and saddle in the theater. Sherman had charged Smith with destroying the Mobile and Ohio Railroad from Okolona, Mississippi, to Meridian and all other military resources along his route. Like Sherman's force to the south, Smith's column had to live off the land. Sherman had warned Smith against getting bogged down in meaningless skirmishes with the enemy and thus jeopardizing their rendezvous at Meridian. Once united, Sherman would decide whether to press on to Selma or return to their bases at Memphis and Vicksburg.

As his force gathered on the outskirts of Memphis, Smith announced that he was ready "to pitch into Forrest wherever I find him." Then he promptly contradicted himself. Receiving word that several units assigned to the expedition had been delayed, he decided to ignore Sherman's timetable and wait for the late arrivals. When they finally appeared, he discovered that many of the men and horses were in no condition for a lightning campaign. To give them time to recover, Smith further delayed his departure until 11 February, thereby ensuring that he would not reach Meridian on time.

Smith's column marched out from Memphis, heading east toward the Mobile and Ohio Railroad and then bearing south into Mississippi. At first, the only resistance the Federal cavalry encountered was an occasional skirmish with a few hundred Mississippi troops under Brig. Gen. Samuel J. Gholson. A sudden deluge turned the roads into quagmires, reducing Smith's rate of advance to a crawl. Adding to the Federals' misery, the temperature plunged below freezing, turning the rain to snow and further impeding the Federal cavalry's march. Destroying everything of military value within reach, Smith's column finally reached Okolona on 18 February. Much to Smith's chagrin, the undisciplined Union troopers were too busy pillaging and damaging Southern property to quicken their pace, even though Meridian still lay one hundred miles to the south. A Union officer noted that "the sky was red with the flames of burning corn and cotton." During the advance from Memphis, the Federal mounted column had averaged just fifteen miles a day.

On 20 February, Smith's column reached West Point, Mississippi, and skirmished with Forrest's cavalry for the first time. Unnerved by false reports that Forrest had been heavily reinforced, Smith decided to return to Memphis, pleading ill health. As further justification, he cited his troopers' lack of discipline, the presence of several thousand fugitive slaves—or "contrabands"—shadowing his column, the swollen creeks and flooded roads, and the ever-present threat of Forrest. Smith also assumed that Sherman had left Meridian and was on his way back to Vicksburg. Grierson tried to convince Smith to press on to Meridian, but the latter was convinced that such a course would merely play into the enemy's hands. On 21 February, he ordered his column to face about and begin the return march to Memphis.

Up to this point, Forrest's much smaller 2,500-man force had fallen back before the Federal advance while seeking an opportunity to strike. Smith's sudden retreat gave Forrest that opportunity. He ordered his command to give chase, and the Confederates drove the Union rear guard through West Point and then outflanked a strong Union position four miles north of town. The Southerners caught up with the Federals in a field just south of Okolona. At 0500 on 22 February, Forrest's cavalry attacked Smith's rear guard, triggering a running fight that lasted most of the day. As the Federals fell back through the streets of Okolona, a portion of Smith's command panicked and, as the panic spread, the retreat became a rout. The demoralized Federals scattered in all directions, abandoning five cannons as well as various other arms and equipment.

General Forrest
(Library of Congress)

About dusk, Union officers managed to rally their men along a ridge on the Ivey farm. The blue-clad troopers fought on foot behind a hastily improvised rail barricade. As the Confederates charged their position, the Federals poured volley after volley into the gray ranks, inflicting numerous casualties and mortally wounding the general's youngest brother, Col. Jeffrey E. Forrest. The elder Forrest rushed to his brother's side, and the young man died in his arms just moments later. Determined to avenge his brother's death, the enraged Forrest ordered a charge and led the way. Inspired by their leader's fearlessness, the Confederates crashed into the Union defensive line, and for a few tense moments, the fighting was hand to hand. Three Federal cavalry regiments then launched a mounted countercharge that halted the Southerners' progress. The Confederates began to give way as they ran out of ammunition, so Forrest ordered his command to break off the attack and rest for the night. The exhausted Federals resumed their retreat.

For the next few days, the Confederates pressed the fleeing Union force but did not engage it. One Federal officer described the remainder of the march as "a weary, disheartening and almost panic-stricken flight, in the greatest disorder and confusion." Passing through areas that they had thoroughly pillaged just days before, the men could find little to eat for either themselves or their mounts. Biting cold and falling snow only compounded their misery. On 26 February, Smith's weary column finally limped into Memphis. The Federals had suffered 388 casualties in the three-day fight from West Point to Okolona, but the expedition had taken such a toll on the remaining men and horses that, for months to come, the Union cavalry in western Tennessee and northern Mississippi would remain largely ineffective. Forrest's cavalry had lost 144 killed, wounded, or missing.

Sherman, meanwhile, had a tough decision to make. Ignorant of Smith's whereabouts and mindful of Grant's injunction to have his command ready to support Banks' Red River expedition, he reluctantly decided to return to Vicksburg rather than pursue Polk into western Alabama. His column departed Meridian on 20 February. Encountering only token resistance along the way, the Federals reached Vicksburg on 3 March. Sherman immediately dispatched part of his force westward to support Banks in the Trans-Mississippi, while sending the balance eastward to Chattanooga for the impending Atlanta Campaign. The commanding general also censured Smith for his disastrous expedition, and the caval-ryman resigned a few months later.

Sherman's Meridian Campaign has often been referred to as a practice run for his campaigns through Georgia and the Carolinas. It certainly bore many similarities to the later raids: marching in two columns, or "wings," to increase mobility and widen the army's reach; employing feints to keep the enemy off balance and unable to attack in strength; destroying rail-roads and other property useful to the Confederate Army; and cutting the "logistical tail" to speed the march and reduce the columns' vulnerability. Sherman's initial use of foraging actually dates back to the Vicksburg Campaign, and it had proved far more effective than he had anticipated. His experience as military governor of Memphis had eliminated whatever qualms he might have had about feeding his troops at the expense of Southern civilians. By early 1864, Sherman had adopted a "hard war" policy in which he deemed the confiscation and destruction of civilian property legitimate acts of war. The Meridian Campaign stands as Sherman's first systematic implementation of that policy.

For all its destructiveness, the Meridian Campaign failed to inflict the kind of long-term damage that Sherman had intended. In addition to rescuing a considerable stockpile of supplies, the Confederates managed to repair the railroads within a month of the raid, and guerrillas continued to harass Federal detachments throughout the region. Worse yet, Forrest's cavalry remained as dangerous as ever. And while Polk had bungled the defense of Meridian, he at least had kept his command intact and ready for more strenuous duty elsewhere. The opportunity for Polk's troops would come later that spring when they would join the Army of Tennessee for the Atlanta Campaign. But according to Maj. Gen. Stephen D. Lee, the commander of Confederate cavalry in Alabama and Mississippi, the demoralizing effect of the Meridian Campaign was undeniable. On 13 March, Lee informed Polk, "The people [of central Mississippi] are badly whipped and much depressed."

On returning to Vicksburg, Sherman not only learned of Smith's disaster, but he also received word that President Abraham Lincoln had appointed Grant general in chief of the U.S. Army and nominated him for promotion to lieutenant general, which Congress duly confirmed on 2 March. Before heading east to assume his new duties, Grant designated Sherman to replace him as commander of the Military Division of the Mississippi. Together, the two men mapped out the Union Army's grand strategy for the upcoming campaign. The main effort would occur on two fronts: Grant would assume the offensive against General Robert E. Lee's army in Virginia, while Sherman would move against Johnston's army in Georgia. Through unified action, the Federals would prevent the two main Confederate armies from reinforcing each other, as they had done the previous year.

Leaving Grant, Sherman traveled to Nashville, Tennessee, and assumed command of the three armies he would lead in the Atlanta Campaign: Thomas' Army of the Cumberland, McPherson's Army of the Tennessee, and the Army of the Ohio under its new commander, Maj. Gen. John M. Schofield. He also oversaw the logistical buildup, keeping a close watch to ensure that only essential personnel and supplies traveled on the single rail line from his main depot at Nashville to his forward base at Chattanooga.

He posted strong guard detachments along the railroad to fend off Forrest's cavalry and other Southern raiders. It remained to be seen who would win the battle of the railroads—the Federals or the Confederates. The outcome might well determine the victor in the Atlanta Campaign.

Fort Pillow, Brice's Crossroads, and Tupelo

While Federal armies assembled in northern Georgia, Confederate cavalry and guerrillas targeted Union garrisons defending the railroads in middle and western Tennessee. The Army of Tennessee relied on these raiders to offset the disparity in manpower and materiel by cutting the railroad and forcing the Federals to detach frontline troops for guard duty. Forrest in particular would become a thorn in Sherman's side as the Union buildup for the Atlanta Campaign progressed in March 1864 (*Map 2*).

Still smarting from the death of his brother at Okolona and incensed by the depredations of Federal soldiers, many of whom were Southern Unionists, Forrest returned to western Tennessee to recruit and conduct another raid to disrupt the Union buildup. He now led an independent cavalry command, as much in recognition of his military skill as it was an acknowledgment of his inability to get along with his superiors. One thing was certain: Forrest seemed to move at will through Union-occupied areas in western Tennessee and Kentucky, wreaking havoc wherever he went. In the meantime, many of the region's Union garrisons had been stripped bare to provide troops for the Atlanta Campaign, leaving a dearth of competent cavalry in Tennessee following Smith's debacle. Sherman was alarmed that Confederate cavalry was operating with impunity throughout the region, but could do little about it for the present. In any event, he reasoned, as long as "that devil Forrest" contented himself with preying on backwater garrisons, preparations for the Atlanta Campaign would continue more or less unimpeded.

Forrest's first two targets were the Federal depots at Union City, Tennessee, and Paducah, Kentucky. On 24 March, Col. William L. Duckworth, one of Forrest's subordinates, attacked Union City with a 500-man force and bluffed the Union commander into surrendering. The Confederates captured the garrison of 480 "renegade Tennesseans" as well as 300 horses and $60,000 in payroll funds. The day after Union City fell, Forrest led 3,000 troopers in an attack on Fort Anderson at Paducah, and though

FORREST COUNTERS
24 March–21 August 1864

Battle

0   25   50
Miles

KENTUCKY
MISSOURI
ARKANSAS
TENNESSEE
MISSISSIPPI
ALABAMA

Ohio R
Mississippi R
Tennessee R
Cumberland R

Cairo
Paducah
FORT ANDERSON
25 Mar
Columbus
Mayfield
Fort Donelson
Fort Henry
UNION CITY
24 Mar
Paris
Johnsonville
Huntingdon
FORT PILLOW
12 Apr
Randolph
Jackson
BOLIVAR
29 Mar
MEMPHIS
21 Aug
Collierville
Corinth
Hernando
Tunica
Helena
Holly Springs
Ripley
BRICE'S CROSSROADS
10 Jun
Baldwyn
OLD TOWN CREEK
15 Jul
Oxford
Pontotoc
Tupelo
TUPELO
14 Jul
Okolona
Aberdeen
Grenada
West Point
Greenwood

Mobile and Ohio RR
Memphis, Clarksville and Louisville RR
Memphis and Ohio RR
Tennessee and Ohio RR
Memphis and Charleston RR
Mississippi and Tennessee RR
Mississippi Central RR
Mobile and Ohio RR

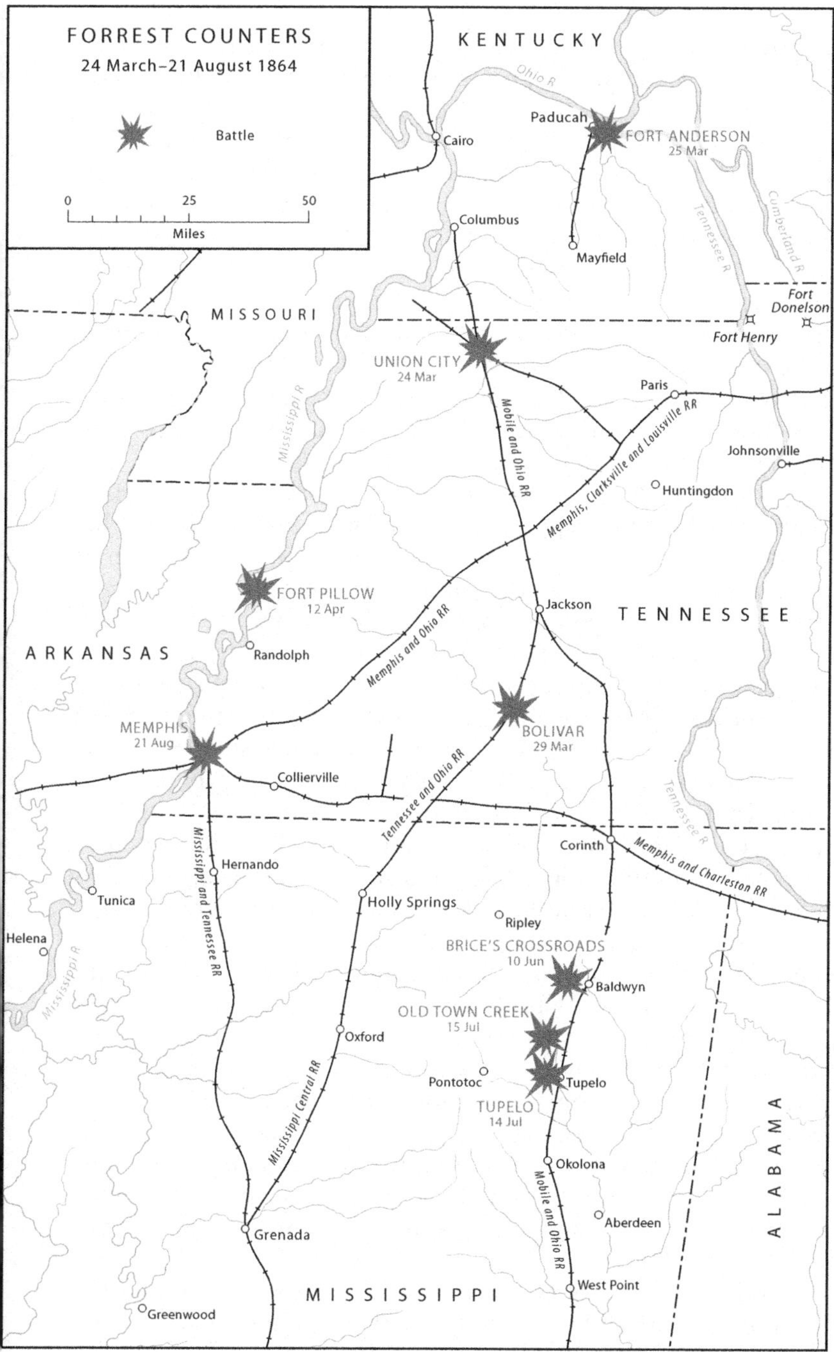

MAP 2

unable to compel the surrender of its 650-man garrison, he did capture a large amount of provisions and medical supplies.

When news of the Confederate attacks on Union City and Paducah reached Memphis, General Grierson—who had succeeded the disgraced W. S. Smith as Sherman's cavalry commander—rushed the only available force northward to challenge Forrest. It happened to be the 6th Tennessee Cavalry, a rowdy band of homegrown Unionists led by the controversial Col. Fielding Hurst. Accusing Hurst and his men of numerous war crimes, Forrest had recently declared them outlaws "not entitled to be treated as prisoners of war." On 29 March, Hurst's command met with defeat near Bolivar, Tennessee, losing its wagon train, fifty thousand rounds of ammunition, and most of its records to the Confederate cavalry under Col. James J. Neely.

Forrest next set his sights on Fort Pillow, which stood on the east bank of the Mississippi River about forty miles above Memphis. The garrison consisted of roughly 550 white Tennessee cavalrymen and black heavy artillerymen. The soldiers were poorly led, largely untrained, and ill-equipped for battle. Although possession of the fort would enable Forrest to impede Union river traffic, he had no intention of holding it. Instead, he wanted to send a message to Tennessee Unionists about the folly of collaborating with the Federals and using freedmen to fight Confederate soldiers.

At dawn on 12 April, about fifteen hundred of Forrest's troopers descended on Fort Pillow and surrounded it, seizing the high ground above the fort. Confederate sharpshooters took a heavy toll on the Union defenders and killed the commanding officer, Col. Lionel F. Booth. Unfortunately for the Federals, rugged terrain and overwhelming Confederate firepower prevented their six cannons and the Union gunboat *New Era* from firing on the Southerners. At 1100, Forrest launched an attack on the fort, which the neophyte garrison repulsed with surprising stubbornness. Forrest then called a truce and demanded the Union garrison's unconditional surrender. The Federal commander, Maj. William Bradford, asked for an hour to consider Forrest's demand, but the latter—aware that the Union transport steamer *Liberty* lurked nearby—granted the Federals just twenty minutes. Bradford refused to surrender, and Forrest ordered his men to storm Fort Pillow.

The Confederates swarmed over the parapet and into the fort, firing on the defenders at point-blank range and driving them down to the river bluffs. In many cases, the victors gave no quarter, shooting unarmed Union soldiers in the act of surrendering. The number of Federals killed was roughly 250, with another 31 dying of their wounds later. Over two-thirds of the fatalities were black soldiers, and only 62 survived the battle. The Confederates lost 14 killed and 86 wounded.

News of the "Fort Pillow Massacre" spread like wildfire throughout the North, becoming a powerful propaganda tool for newspapers and politicians alike. The *Philadelphia Inquirer* condemned the incident as a "Fiendish Slaughter," while the *Chicago Tribune* accused the Confederates at Fort Pillow of "murder" and "butchery." The U.S. Congress Joint Committee on the Conduct of the War conducted an investigation and concluded that "no cruelty which the most fiendish malignity could devise was omitted by these murderers." "Remember Fort Pillow" soon became a popular rallying cry in the North, and USCTs—well aware that the wholesale killing of their black comrades was racially motivated—wore badges emblazoned with the slogan.

The Confederates had held Fort Pillow for just a few hours when Forrest gave the order to evacuate, and his command headed east toward Jackson, Tennessee. In the meantime, Forrest's latest raid convinced Sherman that the incompetent, albeit politically connected, Hurlbut had to go. He was more than a convenient scapegoat. After showing great promise at Shiloh, Hurlbut had risen to corps command, but since then, his alleged drunkenness

Massacre at Fort Pillow
(*Harper's Weekly*, 30 April 1864)

and malfeasance had made him a severe liability. Sherman wanted a general who could at least contain Forrest in western Tennessee during the Atlanta Campaign, and on 18 April he chose Maj. Gen. Cadwallader C. Washburn for the job. He had Grant's trust and seemed more than willing to take on Forrest.

Washburn wasted no time in getting Forrest's attention, engaging the Southern cavalryman in a published correspondence concerning the "Fort Pillow Massacre." Bristling at Washburn's public rebukes, Forrest condemned the vows that black troops in Memphis allegedly had made to avenge Fort Pillow by giving no quarter to his men. Far more damaging to Forrest—and other Confederate commanders—was General Grant's insistence that black soldiers and their white officers be accorded fair treatment in prisoner exchanges. On 17 April, just five days after the "Fort Pillow Massacre," Grant directed that the exchanges cease unless these conditions were met, thereby weakening the numerically inferior Confederate Army still further. The suspension of prisoner exchanges impeded Forrest's ability to replace his losses just as the Atlanta Campaign got under way in early May.

On 31 May, Washburn directed Brig. Gen. Samuel D. Sturgis to march into northeastern Mississippi and engage Forrest to prevent another raid into middle Tennessee to cut Sherman's vulnerable supply lines. Just one month earlier, Sturgis had attempted to bring Forrest to battle and had come up empty-handed. On this expedition, he took three infantry brigades under Col. William L. McMillen and two cavalry brigades under General Grierson, altogether about 8,000 men, 22 cannons, and 250 wagons. Sturgis' force included a contingent of USCTs who wore "Remember Fort Pillow" badges. On 1 June, Sturgis set out from

General Sturgis
(Library of Congress)

Memphis, and a downpour quickly turned the roads into quagmires. The rain continued to fall for several days. On 8 June, the sodden Federal column slogged into Ripley, Mississippi, having covered just fifty miles in one week.

As Sherman had guessed, Forrest was about to embark on another raid into middle Tennessee when he learned of the Sturgis expedition. He immediately turned his back on the Tennessee River and led his 4,800 men toward Tupelo, Mississippi. Rather than wait for reinforcements from General S. D. Lee, Forrest relied on his expert knowledge of the terrain and hastily arranged an ambush for Sturgis along the banks of Tishomingo Creek near an intersection known as Brice's Crossroads. Although heavily outnumbered, Forrest hoped to strike the Union column as it crossed the narrow bridge over the creek and destroy it in detail.

At dawn on 10 June, Sturgis' command broke camp and headed southeast toward Brice's Crossroads, with Grierson's cavalry in the advance. Around 0930, the Union horsemen collided with Forrest's lead brigade about a half mile east of the crossroads. The two sides fought dismounted, and by 1100, the Confederates began to press the Federals back. Grierson requested infantry support, and Sturgis ordered McMillen's foot soldiers to advance at the double-quick. Although a gap opened in Grierson's line, the Confederates were too overcome by the heat and humidity to exploit it, and both sides halted for a much-needed rest. The Union infantry began to arrive around 1330, but the men were exhausted from jogging five miles under a blazing midday sun, and numerous stragglers fell out during the grueling march.

Having fought for over three hours in the sweltering heat, Grierson's cavalry began to waver as the Federal infantry went into position, with Sturgis forming a semicircular line just east of Brice's Crossroads. After two hours of continuous fighting along this position, Forrest decided to strike. He directed his chief of artillery, Capt. John W. Morton, to advance his battery to within point-blank range of McMillen's line and open fire with double rounds of canister. Forrest knew that he was risking the loss of Morton's rifled guns, but his gamble paid off. Morton's four cannons inflicted heavy casualties on the Federals and spread fear and confusion in their ranks. Then he sent detachments sweeping around each of the Union flanks. At about 1700, Forrest launched a general assault that shattered Sturgis' line and stampeded the Union soldiers. The road leading to the bridge over Tishomingo Creek became clogged with fleeing troops, abandoned wagons, and discarded weapons and equipment. Worse yet, a bottleneck formed at the bridge itself, as masses of panicked men and horses struggled to get across. One of the few bright spots in the Federal rout was a skillful delaying action conducted by Sturgis' rear guard—two regiments of USCTs under Col. Edward Bouton.

The extent of the Union disaster is revealed by the losses sustained. The Federals abandoned 16 artillery pieces and 176 wagons laden with ammunition and other supplies, and they suffered over 2,200 casualties, including 1,600 prisoners. The Confederates lost about 500 casualties. Sturgis' shattered column staggered back into Memphis on 13 June, covering the same distance in retreat in less than half the time the column had taken to reach Brice's Crossroads. News of yet another rout at Forrest's hands filled both the Northern public and the Union high command with indignation and apprehension.

One month later, Sherman directed Washburn to send another expedition after the South's most elusive cavalryman, and he chose Maj. Gen. Andrew J. Smith for the mission. A U.S. Military Academy graduate and a Mexican War veteran, Smith had just returned from Banks' unsuccessful Red River expedition, where he had nonetheless served with distinction. Sherman wanted Smith to "follow Forrest to the death if it costs 10,000 lives and breaks the Treasury. There will never be peace in Tennessee till Forrest is dead."

General A. J. Smith
(Library of Congress)

Leading a force of fourteen thousand infantry and cavalry and twenty-four pieces of artillery, Smith set out for Tupelo on 5 July. One week later, he collided with Forrest's cavalry near Pontotoc, Mississippi, about eighteen miles west of Tupelo. Forrest had deployed on a hill, hoping to lure Smith into making an attack, but the Union commander refused to take the bait and headed east toward Tupelo instead. Smith's decision to avoid battle surprised Forrest, who had left the road to Tupelo unguarded. He immediately set out in pursuit, his advance skirmishing with the Union rear guard for most of the day. That evening, Smith occupied the high ground at Harrisburg, a hamlet about one mile west of Tupelo. He sent Grierson's cavalry into Tupelo to damage the Mobile and Ohio Railroad, while his foot soldiers further strengthened their position by building earth and fence rail breastworks.

In the meantime, S. D. Lee—newly promoted to lieutenant general—joined Forrest with two thousand additional troopers, having ridden from Okolona, where he had expected to fight Smith's force. The Confederates now had seven thousand cavalry, roughly one-half the soldiers Smith had. Lee recommended that they attack the next morning. Suffering from an outbreak of boils, Forrest refused Lee's offer to let him remain in command, saying that Lee was his superior. Then he gave his frank assessment of Lee's plan. Having made a personal reconnaissance of the Union position, Forrest stated that his men would have to advance across open ground against a vastly larger foe shielded by strong fortifications. Instead, he suggested that they simply wait and force Smith to attack them. But Lee would not be dissuaded—the assault would begin as early as possible on 14 July.

Due to miscommunication, the Confederate frontal assault on the Federal line was disjointed, with individual brigades advancing piecemeal into a devastating barrage of musketry and artillery. The Union defenders easily repulsed the ill-timed attacks and inflicted heavy losses. Seeing that the assaults on the Federal right and center had failed, Forrest withheld his division on the Union left to avoid taking additional casualties in a futile attack. When Lee learned of

General S. D. Lee
(Library of Congress)

this, he became angry. "In doing as you did," he told Forrest, "you failed to carry out the plan of battle agreed on."

As the Confederates withdrew from the battlefield, Smith's infantry commander, Brig. Gen. Joseph A. Mower, launched a counterattack, driving off or capturing the few remaining Southerners. Mower had his men gather the prisoners and the wounded and collect the Confederates' abandoned weapons and equipment. By this time, several Union soldiers had collapsed with sunstroke, inducing Mower to return to the main line. That evening, the Federals set fire to some of the buildings in Harrisburg; Confederate artillery crews used the flames to direct their shells at the Union position.

The Battle of Tupelo had cost the Confederates dearly. They lost 1,298 killed, wounded, or missing—nearly 20 percent of their total strength. The Federals sustained 648 casualties, including one of Smith's brigade commanders, Col. Alexander Wilkin, who was killed in action. Owing to a lack of wagons and ambulances, Smith had to leave forty of his severely wounded men behind at Tupelo.

Smith had won a clear victory and had lost relatively few men, but he learned that most of his rations had spoiled in the midsummer heat and his ammunition was running low. He therefore decided to break contact with the Confederates and return to Memphis. On 15 July, Smith began marching northward. Forrest now had the opportunity he had sought to pursue a retreating foe, and Lee was only too happy to turn over command of the pursuit to him. Once again, Forrest's advance skirmished with the Union rear guard, and before long, his entire force became heavily engaged with the Federals at Old Town Creek a few miles north of Harrisburg.

The Confederates succeeded in driving Grierson's cavalry, but were in turn forced back by the Union infantry. During the seesaw fight, two of Forrest's brigade commanders were severely wounded, and Forrest himself received a painful wound in the right foot that sidelined him for three weeks. The Southerners fell back to Harrisburg and regrouped, enabling the Federals to withdraw unopposed into Tennessee. At first Smith was criticized for not destroying Forrest's cavalry, but as time passed, it became apparent that he had done enough damage to prevent the Confederates from cutting Sherman's supply lines.

But Forrest would not remain inactive for long. On 21 August, he launched a raid on Memphis, exploiting the city's weak defenses and the Federal garrison's low state of readiness. Emerging from the early morning fog, Forrest and about fifteen hundred Confederate troopers rode into the "Bluff City," after encountering only token resistance from Union pickets. They soon split up into detachments and then galloped through the streets, firing and yelling "like Comanches," recalled a participant. One detachment under Forrest's brother, Lt. Col. Jesse Forrest, attempted to bag General Washburn, while a second detachment under another brother, Capt. William Forrest, went after General Hurlbut. Although both Union generals eluded capture, many of their staff officers became prisoners, and the Confederates made off with Washburn's uniform. This prompted Hurlbut to quip, "They removed me from command because I couldn't keep Forrest out of West Tennessee, and now Washburn can't keep him out of his own bedroom." The men of Captain Forrest's squad also tried to break into Irving Block Prison to liberate their captive comrades but lacked the numbers to overwhelm the prison guard. After several hours of mayhem, the various detachments reunited about 0900, and Forrest departed Memphis with six hundred prisoners and other spoils.

Thus far in 1864, Forrest's cavalry and other Confederate raiders had repeatedly embarrassed Union occupation forces in the Western Theater, exposing the vulnerability of the Union logistical network. These raids compelled Sherman to detach veteran troops for guard duty at a time when the Federal commander needed every man on the front line.

Atlanta and Its Aftermath

While the various Union expeditions from Memphis kept Forrest occupied in northeastern Mississippi, Sherman's army group advanced into the heart of Georgia, executing a series of skillful turning movements against the Army of Tennessee under General Johnston. At the start of the Atlanta Campaign, Sherman's force boasted 97,000 troops and 254 guns, while Johnston's army numbered 60,000 soldiers and 144 guns. Despite the numerical disadvantage, the defensive-minded Johnston made the Federals pay in blood for the ground they gained, most notably at Kennesaw Mountain on 27 June. But he could not stop them, and by mid-July, the three Union armies were encircling Atlanta, the last major transportation and manufacturing center in the Deep South. Convinced that Johnston intended to give up Atlanta without a fight, President Davis replaced him with the more aggressive General John Bell Hood on 17 July. In three hard-fought battles that took a heavy toll on his army, Hood failed to break the Federals' stranglehold on the city. The fall of Atlanta on 2 September, following the Battle of Jonesboro, boosted flagging Northern morale and ensured Lincoln's reelection that November.

General Hood
(Hal Jesperson)

But the war in the West was far from over. The Army of Tennessee, about forty thousand strong, was still dangerous, if only a shadow of its former self. Hood had moved his army to Palmetto, Georgia, about twenty-five miles southwest of Atlanta, to give it a much-needed rest. In mid-August, he had sent Maj. Gen. Joseph Wheeler and most of the Army of Tennessee's cavalry on a raid to cut Sherman's supply lines in Tennessee. But Wheeler had failed to stop the flow of Union supplies, and his absence had left Hood blind. In late September, Wheeler rejoined the Army of Tennessee, while Forrest launched another raid into middle Tennessee. Hood, meanwhile, left Palmetto on 29 September, crossed the Chattahoochee River, and led the Army of Tennessee northward to strike the Western and Atlantic Railroad, Sherman's supply line between Chattanooga and Atlanta. To deal with Forrest, Sherman sent General Thomas and two divisions to Nashville.

On 5 October, Hood detached one of his divisions to attack Allatoona, Georgia, the main Union depot between Chattanooga and Atlanta, and the Federals barely managed to hold out in a small yet fierce battle that resulted in over fourteen hundred total casualties out of fifty-three hundred combatants. The Confederates met with greater success at Dalton, Georgia, where an 800-man garrison surrendered without a fight. Sherman then pursued Hood's army along the railroad until mid-October, when it veered westward into northern Alabama. Abandoning the chase at Gaylesville, Alabama, Sherman turned his attention to defending Tennessee and resuming his advance through Georgia. He sent two corps to

General Thomas
(Library of Congress)

Chattanooga and placed them under Thomas' command while retaining four corps for his next campaign (*See Map 3*).

Bearing in mind the lessons of the Meridian Campaign, Sherman proposed to Grant a "March to the Sea" in which he would sever his cumbersome supply lines, march his army 250 miles to the Georgia coast, and capture the port city of Savannah. Sherman's army group would live off the land while damaging both the Confederate infrastructure and Southern morale. "I can make the march, and make Georgia howl," Sherman assured Grant. "If we can march a well-appointed army right through this territory," he argued, "it is a demonstration to the world, foreign and domestic, that we have a power which [Jefferson] Davis cannot resist. This may not be war, but rather statesmanship." Grant gave his approval, and Sherman began preparing for the March to the Sea, trusting Thomas to defeat Hood while he headed to Savannah.

It is ironic that President Davis had made reference to Sherman in a speech given during a recent visit to Georgia. He had predicted that Sherman would suffer a disaster similar to what had befallen Napoleon in Russia some fifty years earlier. "We will flank General Sherman out of Atlanta," Davis had declared, "tear up the railroad and cut off his supplies, and make Atlanta a perfect Moscow of defeat to the Federal army." Davis had made the circuitous rail journey from Richmond, Virginia, to discuss strategy with Hood, but he also gave speeches along the way to boost civilian morale, which was much shaken by the fall of Atlanta.

Hood had come under widespread criticism since assuming command of the Army of Tennessee in mid-July. While no one questioned his courage or dedication, numerous critics—including many of the general's subordinates—accused him of squandering the lives of his men in reckless assaults that were doomed to fail. Davis, however, decided to retain Hood as commander of the Army of Tennessee.

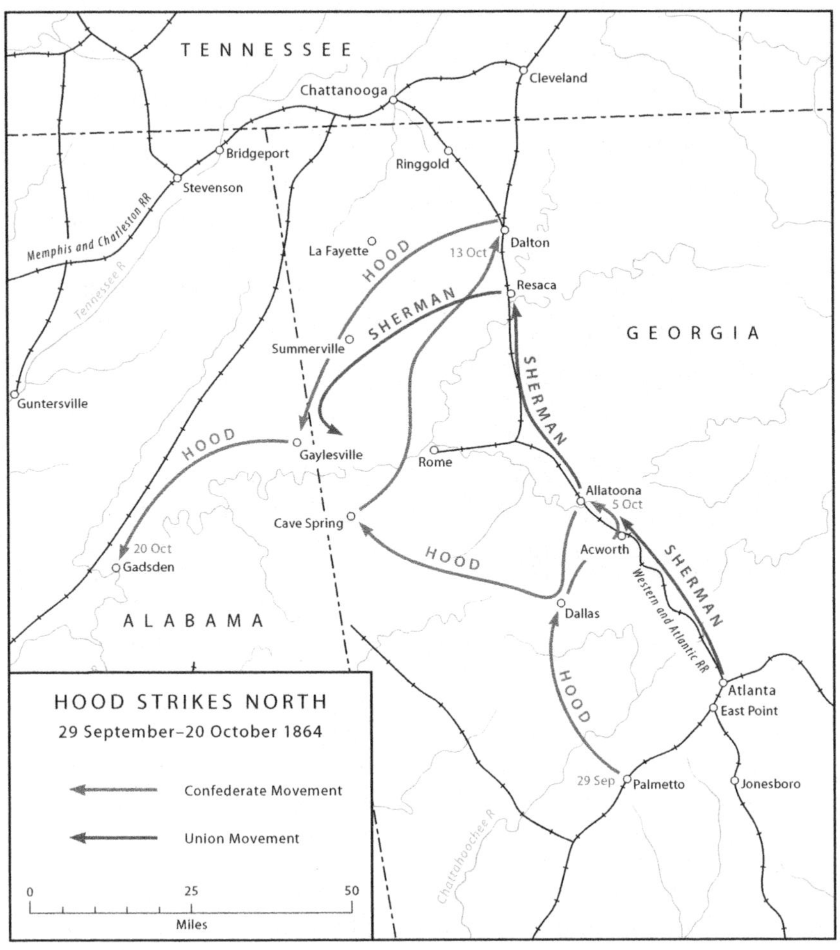

MAP 3

He also approved the general's plan to cut the Union supply line in northern Georgia and force Sherman to fight a battle on ground of Hood's own choosing.

During the march into northern Alabama, Hood decided on a far more audacious plan that involved defeating Thomas at Nashville before he could concentrate his scattered forces. Once that was accomplished, Hood would be free to enter Kentucky—perhaps sweeping as far north as the Ohio River—or head east to join Lee's army in Virginia.

On 20 October, Hood reached Gadsden, Alabama, where he briefed General Pierre G. T. Beauregard on his new plan. The Confederate War Department had just appointed Beauregard commander of the Military Division of the West, and as such, he was Hood's superior. The Creole approved Hood's plan and began collecting supplies for the Army of Tennessee, ignoring the fact that a similar offensive two years earlier had failed under far more favorable circumstances.

The Johnsonville Raid

While Hood embarked on a new campaign, Forrest launched yet another daring raid into Tennessee to interdict Sherman's supply lines. The window of opportunity was closing fast, for within a month Sherman would sever his own supply lines, leaving Forrest power-less to interfere with his campaign to "make Georgia howl." Unable in a previous raid to cut Sherman's supply line between Nashville and Chattanooga, he decided to strike at a more remote point. The objective was the Union depot at Johnsonville, Tennessee, located on the east bank of the Tennessee River about seventy-five miles west of Nashville. Most Federal supplies traveling south on the Tennessee went to Johnsonville, where they were sent by railroad to Nashville. Starting from Corinth, Mississippi, with fewer than three thousand troopers, Forrest reached Johnsonville on 3 November. Thanks to the capture of a Union gunboat and steamer, he briefly commanded a joint Army-Navy task force—that is, until attacking Federal gunboats forced the Confederates to abandon one vessel and scuttle the other (*See Map 4*).

Forrest found the depot well-defended. Three Union gunboats guarded the river approaches, and a 2,000-man garrison—including about 800 "armed quartermaster's employees"—supported by twelve guns occupied a hilltop fortification that overlooked the facility. The Confederates spent much of 3–4 November positioning their artil-lery. The time was well spent, for on the afternoon and evening of 4 November, the Southern batteries managed to cripple the gunboats and set fire to Federal steamboats and barges at the wharf without being fired on. To prevent any ships or supplies from falling into enemy hands, the Union commander ordered his men to burn all vessels not already ablaze. "By night," Forrest later recalled, "the wharf for nearly one mile up and down the river presented one solid sheet of flame." Forrest's Johnsonville raid ranks as one of the most destructive of the war. The Federals estimated that the total property loss came to $2.2 million, including one warehouse, four gunboats,

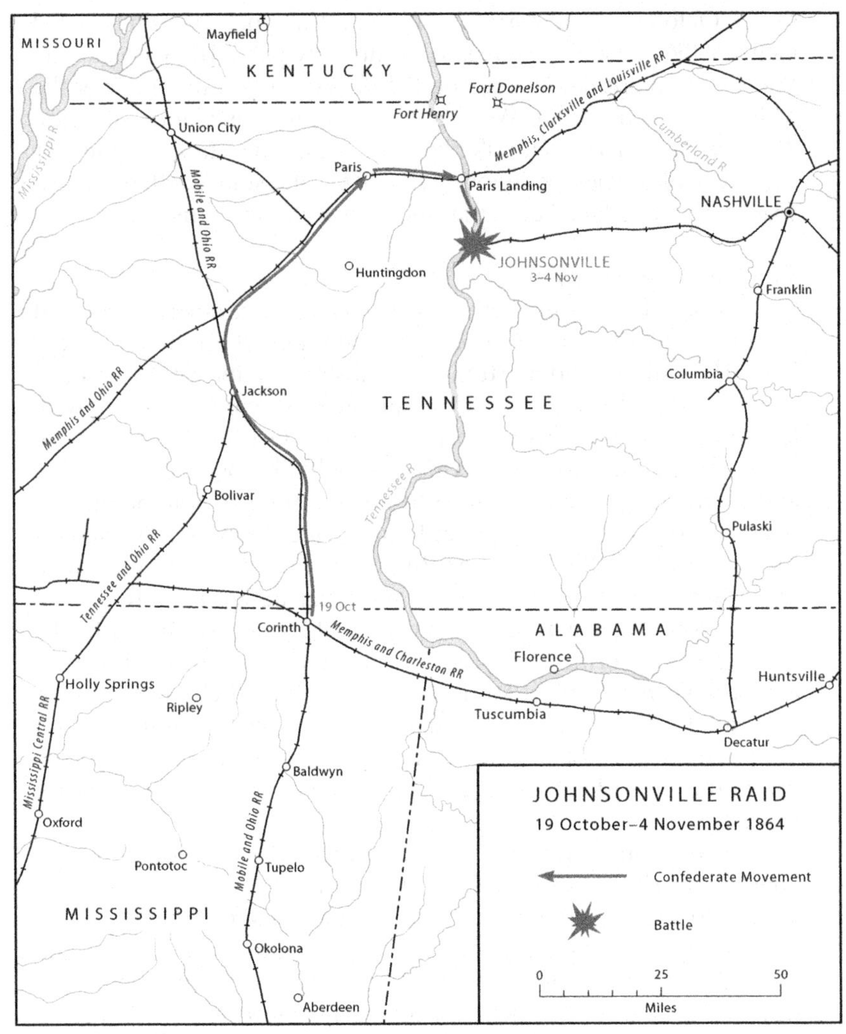

Map 4

fourteen transports, twenty barges, and twenty-six guns. Forrest reported that his command captured one hundred fifty Federals, while his own loss for the entire raid totaled two men killed and nine wounded. He had no difficulty evading the units that Thomas sent in pursuit after news of the disaster reached Nashville.

On 22 October, while Forrest rode north toward Johnsonville, Hood left Gadsden, heading west to find a safe place to cross the Tennessee River. The march was a miserable one. "We were cut off from our rations," recalled one Confederate, "ragged, shoeless, hatless, and many even without blankets; the pangs of hunger and physical exhaustion were now added to our sufferings." Hood passed up the crossing of the Tennessee at Guntersville because he claimed to lack the cavalry needed to protect his wagon train in Tennessee. He reached the Federal depot at Decatur, Alabama, on 26 October, but the garrison refused to surrender. After making a reconnaissance, he deemed the facility not worth the losses he would likely incur in a frontal assault. Hood pushed on to Tuscumbia, Alabama, where the shallows would prevent Union gunboats from contesting his crossing of the Tennessee. His weary army arrived there on the last day of October. Hood directed the army's commissary and quartermaster officers to amass twenty days' worth of supplies at Tuscumbia, but their efforts were hampered by a break in the Memphis and Charleston Railroad, which required a fifteen-mile trek by wagon. Worse yet, torrential rains made the roads almost impassable (*See Map 5*).

Beauregard, meanwhile, directed Hood to send Wheeler's cavalry into Georgia to harass Sherman's army group, and he summoned Forrest's cavalry to join Hood's army. But Forrest was in the middle of his Johnsonville raid when Beauregard's message reached him on 30 October. While waiting for Forrest at Tuscumbia, Hood collected supplies for the coming campaign, and Beauregard attempted to rebuild the railroad to facilitate the effort. By the time Forrest reached the Army of Tennessee on 14 November, Hood had only seven days' provisions on hand, far less than the twenty days' supply he deemed essential. But he realized that time was growing short and ordered the army to cross the Tennessee River on 14–15 November. When word arrived that Sherman had begun his March to the Sea, Hood discussed the situation with Beauregard and decided that an offensive into middle Tennessee was his only viable option. On 21 November, the Army of Tennessee set out from Florence, Alabama, for Nashville. Winter had come early to middle Tennessee, and the Confederate soldiers, many of them barefoot and clad in little more than rags, suffered keenly as they marched over frozen roads amid harsh winds mixed with sleet and snow.

KENTUCKY
Fort Donelson
Fort Henry
Clarksville
Gallatin
Cumberland R
Memphis, Clarksville and Louisville RR
Tennessee R
Johnsonville
Clifton
THOMAS
NASHVILLE
2 Dec
Harpeth R
FORREST
FRANKLIN
30 Nov
THIRD
MURFREESBORO
7 Dec
Duck R
TENNESSEE
SPRING HILL
29 Nov
Columbia
Nashville and Chattanooga RR
CHEATHAM
S. D. LEE
STEWART
SCHOFIELD
Shelbyville
24 Nov
Pulaski
Tennessee and Alabama Central RR
Stevenson
MISSISSIPPI
21 Nov
Florence
Bainbridge
Huntsville
Memphis and Charleston RR
Tennessee R
14–15 Nov
HOOD
Tuscumbia
31 Oct
Decatur
26 Oct
HOOD
Guntersville
ALABAMA
Gadsden
22 Oct
Black Warrior R

TENNESSEE CAMPAIGN
22 October–7 December 1864
Confederate Movement
Union Movement
Battle
0   25   50
Miles

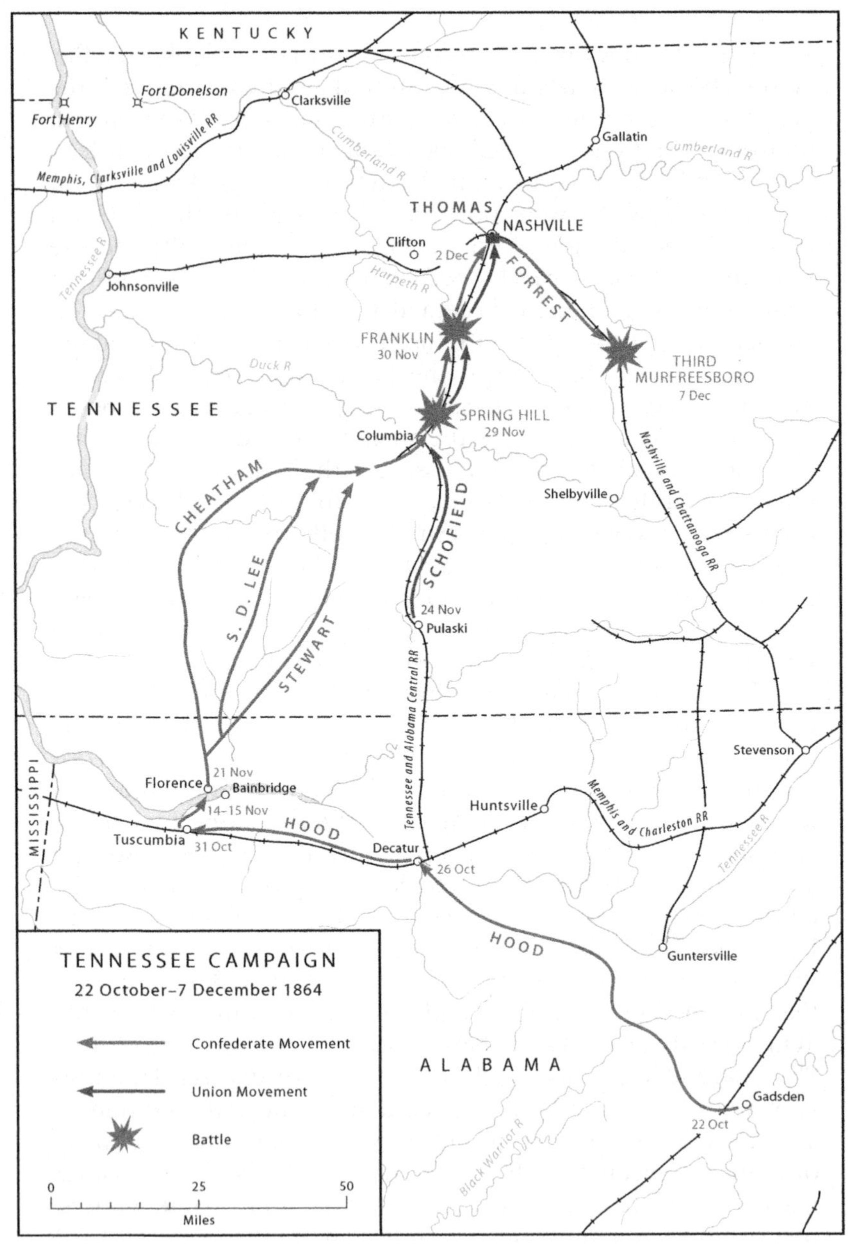

MAP 5

At Nashville, meanwhile, General Thomas attempted to concentrate his forces before Hood could strike. He had about sixty thousand troops scattered throughout Kentucky and Tennessee. Seventy miles to the south, the Union IV and XXIII Corps under General Schofield, twenty-six thousand strong, awaited Hood's advance at Pulaski, Tennessee. Thomas' cavalry commander, Brig. Gen. James H. Wilson, had about four thousand troopers with Schofield, but his command was in desperate need of horses and equipment. Another ten thousand soldiers of the XVI Corps under General A. J. Smith were en route from Missouri. To buy time for their arrival, Thomas instructed Schofield to delay the Army of Tennessee's advance, and he ordered Wilson to keep Forrest away from the railroads. He also called in his garrisons and outposts to prevent them from being gobbled up by the Confederates.

As Hood's army approached from the southwest, Schofield withdrew from Pulaski on 24 November and marched toward Columbia thirty miles to the north. Forrest, meanwhile, sent his six thousand cavalry on a wide sweep to cut off Schofield's retreat. But the Federal infantry had arrived well ahead of the Confederate cavalry and were already dug in along the Duck River.

General Schofield
(Library of Congress)

General Wilson
(Library of Congress)

Borrowing a page from Sherman's Atlanta Campaign tactics, Hood launched a flanking maneuver around the Union left with the bulk of his army, while two infantry divisions kept the Federals occupied at Columbia. On the morning of 29 November, Forrest briefly clashed with Wilson's Union cavalry, drawing it away from Schofield's column, and then made a dash for the village of Spring Hill, Tennessee, about ten miles to the north. In the meantime, Schofield ordered his wagon train to withdraw toward Spring Hill on the Columbia Pike. The IV Corps under Maj. Gen. David S. Stanley was escorting the Federals' eight hundred wagons and forty pieces of artillery when Stanley learned that the Union garrison at Spring Hill was under attack. He passed the word to the commander of his lead brigade, Col. Emerson Opdycke, who gave the order to advance up the turnpike at a run. The race to Spring Hill was on.

When Forrest's troopers reached Spring Hill, two IV Corps brigades were waiting for them, and a third was on the way. The Confederate cavalry, fighting dismounted, lacked the numbers to drive the Federal infantry. They could only watch as the Union wagon train rumbled through Spring Hill and went into park just north of town. At 1500, as the Confederate infantry approached to within a few miles of Spring Hill, Hood directed that Maj. Gen. Benjamin F. Cheatham deploy his corps east of Spring Hill on Forrest's left. Cheatham was to advance west toward the Columbia Pike and the Union column, and then wheel north, driving the enemy through Spring Hill, while Lt. Gen. Alexander P. Stewart's corps waited in reserve to support Cheatham's attack if needed.

By the time Cheatham's lead division under Maj. Gen. Patrick R. Cleburne arrived at Spring Hill one hour later, Hood had modified his orders. He directed Cleburne to head west toward the Columbia Pike and then swing south to drive

General Cheatham
(Library of Congress)

the Union column back toward Columbia. Hood's intent was to prevent Schofield's XXIII Corps at Columbia from reaching Stanley's IV Corps at Spring Hill. Hood issued the same order to Maj. Gen. William B. Bate, whose division formed on Cleburne's left. Cheatham was unaware of the change in orders, however, and just before Cleburne launched his assault, he reiterated his order to "take" Spring Hill. He also directed Bate to conform to Cleburne's movements, in effect countermanding Hood's order. The conflicting orders created much confusion among the two division commanders and their staff officers, but after some discussion, they decided to heed Cheatham's order to attack toward Spring Hill. Overrunning a Union infantry brigade, Cleburne's three brigades came face-to-face with eighteen Federal cannons that General Stanley had deployed south of town. The guns blazed forth in the fading light, sending the Confederates scurrying for cover. Nightfall brought an end to Cleburne's assault. The action had cost the Federals about 400 casualties and the Confederates roughly 250 losses.

Instead of deploying across the Columbia Pike to block Schofield's approach route to Spring Hill, the Confederates went into camp along the roadside, confident that they had trapped the Federals south of town and could dispose of them in the morning. Complacency and miscommunication among the Confederate high command enabled Schofield's column to march past in the darkness without being challenged. Historian Wiley Sword describes the Union escape at Spring Hill "as one of the greatest missed opportunities of the entire war."

General Cleburne
(Library of Congress)

Hood awoke to learn that the Federals had slipped past his army during the night. He was furious. That morning he summoned his senior subordinates to a conference and lashed out at them for allowing the enemy to escape. Forrest's cavalry, meanwhile, pursued the Union rear guard—namely Opdycke's brigade—toward the village of Franklin, Tennessee, about a dozen miles north of Spring Hill. The Army of Tennessee's infantry followed a few miles behind the cavalry.

Before dawn on 30 November, General Schofield—exhausted from a sleepless night in the saddle—rode into Franklin, only to discover that his wagon train had nowhere to cross the Harpeth River north of town. Although the Harpeth was fordable at several points and the railroad bridge remained intact, the wagon bridge was in ruins. Worse yet, Schofield had been compelled to abandon his pontoon bridge at Columbia, and Thomas had not yet sent a replacement. He therefore decided to rebuild the wagon bridge and to plank over the railroad bridge, meanwhile using the fords to cross most of the artillery, with one division of the IV Corps serving as escort. As if Schofield needed further incentive to remain at Franklin, Thomas sent several telegrams that day urging him to hold Hood's army there for as long as possible.

Schofield accordingly directed that the XXIII Corps and two divisions of the IV Corps deploy south of Franklin. He placed Brig. Gen. Jacob D. Cox, his most trusted subordinate, in temporary command of the XXIII Corps and in overall command of the defensive line. Cox in turn designated Brig. Gen. James W. Reilly as acting commander of his XXIII Corps division. Reilly's troops held the sector running from the Harpeth westward to the Columbia Pike, Brig. Gen. Thomas H. Ruger's XXIII Corps division occupied the position from the Columbia Pike to the Carter's Creek Pike, and Brig. Gen. Nathan Kimball's IV Corps division defended the line from the Carter's Creek Pike northward to the Harpeth. Wilson's cavalry covered the area east of the river. The Union force numbered about twenty-seven thousand soldiers.

Schofield also directed that the existing fortifications south of town—constructed in 1863 and now somewhat deteriorated—be improved and expanded under Cox's supervision. The men began by piling up a long row of logs, fence rails, and planks taken from the cotton gin on the Fountain Branch Carter farm. Then they tossed countless shovelfuls of soil onto the wood skeleton, and as the earthen mound grew, deep trenches formed on either side of the breastwork. Next, they placed thick head logs on top of the parapet, leaving a slit to fire their weapons through. On the left of the Union line, soldiers stacked numerous tough and thorny Osage orange hedges in front of their works as obstructions.

Along the right and center of the line, felled apple and locust trees served the same purpose. By noon, the Federals had constructed a mile-long, crescent-shaped entrenchment that averaged about five feet high and four feet thick, fronted by a dense abatis consisting of tangled hedges and tree branches. Running from northwest to southeast, the Union fortifications covered the southern and western approaches into Franklin, and both flanks rested on the Harpeth River. Their labors finished, the men were free to eat and sleep and bask in the warmth of a bright Indian summer afternoon.

General Cox
(Library of Congress)

About half a mile south of the main line, Brig. Gen. George D. Wagner deployed two brigades of his IV Corps division on either side of the Columbia Pike. Cox had instructed him to delay the Confederate advance and withdraw to the main line if pressed. Wagner apparently chose to interpret Cox's order as an injunction to hold his position to the last, angrily telling one of his brigade commanders to have his sergeants fix bayonets and force the men to do their duty.

In any event, Colonel Opdycke, the commander of Wagner's third brigade, refused to occupy the salient and promptly led his troops back to the main line and placed them in reserve. In a heated exchange with Wagner, he explained that his men needed a breather after their lengthy stint as the army's rear guard. The strong-willed Opdycke thus left the equally stubborn Wagner no choice but to accept his brigade's retired position as an accomplished fact.

A few miles south of Wagner's line, the Army of Tennessee advanced toward Franklin in two long gray and butternut columns, one column winding along the Lewisburg Pike to the southeast and the other taking the Columbia Pike to the south. Hood reached Winstead Hill about 1300 and scanned the Union position with his field glasses. What he saw pleased him immensely: a line of temporary fieldworks in front of the town and a long wagon train jamming the enemy's line of retreat.

Hood thereupon decided to launch a frontal assault and drive the Federals into the Harpeth River. He called a council of war and asked for his subordinates' opinions. Forrest disagreed vehemently with Hood's plan and offered to flank the enemy out of Franklin with his cavalry and one strong division of infantry. Cheatham and Cleburne observed that the Federal works appeared formidable and that attacking them across two miles of open ground could prove costly. But Hood would not be swayed—he was determined to eradicate the Army of Tennessee's aversion to frontal attacks, stemming from the army's dependence on earthworks instilled by his predecessor, General Johnston. He stated that he preferred to attack the Yankees at Franklin, where they had only a few hours to prepare, rather than at Nashville, where they had spent the past three years strengthening their defenses.

At 1600, General Cheatham ordered a flag dropped on Winstead Hill, signaling the attack to begin. Stewart's corps moved forward on the right and Cheatham's corps advanced on the left, while Forrest's cavalry followed on the infantry's flanks. Col. Ellison Capers, the commander of the 24th South Carolina Infantry, later recalled the Army of Tennessee's procession over the open fields south of Franklin. "Bands were playing," he wrote, "general and staff officers were riding in front of and between the lines, a hundred battle-flags were waving in the smoke of battle, and bursting shells were wreathing the air in great circles of smoke, while twenty[-seven] thousand brave men were marching in perfect order against the foe."

The Confederates employed minimal artillery support, for most of the army's guns were with Lee's corps at the rear of the column. In contrast, Union artillery on the main line and at Fort Granger east of Franklin—where Schofield had an excellent view of the battle—pounded the Confederates with shell and solid shot from the outset. At first the Southern brigades marched in columns to present as narrow a front to the Federals as possible. When they came to within a half mile of Wagner's line, the Confederates formed into line of battle for the final push (*Map 6*).

The heavy musketry along Wagner's line staggered the Southern advance, but the vast gray and butternut line

NASHVILLE PIKE
Fort Granger
Harpeth R.
FRANKLIN
LEWISBURG PIKE
WILSON
Harpeth R.
KIMBALL
COX
REILLY
LORING
FORREST
OPDYCKE
Carter
WALTHALL
RUGER
FRENCH
STEWART
WAGNER
Tennessee and Alabama Central RR
CLEBURNE
BROWN
CHEATHAM
CARTER'S CREEK PIKE
BATE
COLUMBIA PIKE
CHALMERS

BATTLE OF FRANKLIN
30 November 1864

Confederate Position
Confederate Attack
Union Position
Union Retreat
Union Counterattack
Union Entrenchments

0   ½   1
Mile

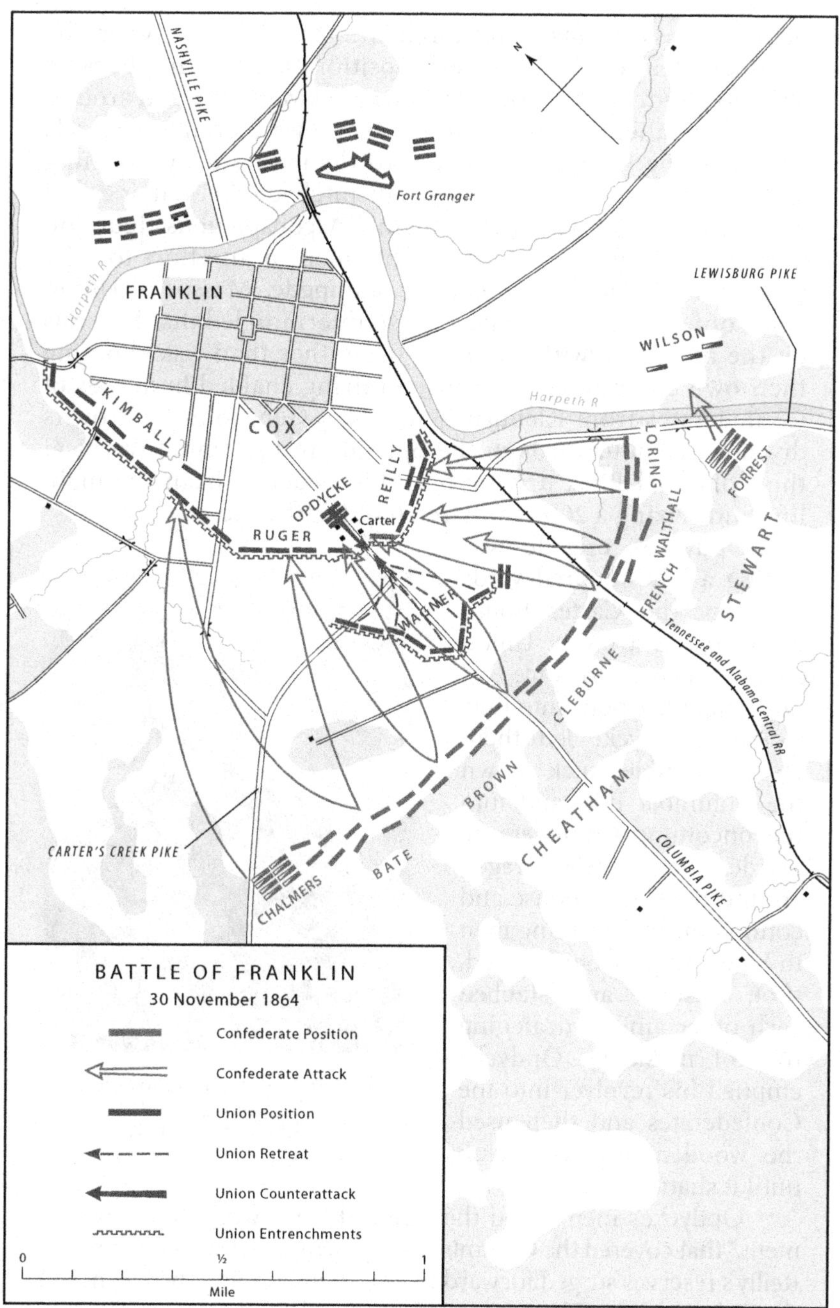

Map 6

paused, dressed ranks, and lurched forward again. When the Confederates reached Wagner's position, the fighting became hand to hand, but the Southerners soon swept over and around the Union salient, capturing more than seven hundred Federals and pursuing the remainder toward the main line. Onrushing men in gray screamed the eerie, high-pitched rebel yell or called out, "Go into the works with them!" A conspicuous figure on horseback, Wagner rode among his men in an effort to rally them but was unable to halt the stampede. Masses of Union and Confederate soldiers became so intermingled that Federals on the main line withheld their fire rather than risk shooting their own comrades. This pause in firing enabled hundreds of Confederates from Cleburne's and Maj. Gen. John C. Brown's divisions to pour through the opening in the Union works at the Columbia Pike, driving back the Federals from the main line and seizing a 200-yard stretch of fortifications.

Opdycke's brigade was resting a few hundred yards north of the Carter house when panic-stricken Union soldiers began to race by. Ordering his troops into line, Colonel Opdycke led them at the double-quick down the Columbia Pike and into the oncoming Confederates. A desperate melee raged around the Carter house and cotton gin, as screaming men in blue and gray bludgeoned, shot, slashed, and stabbed each other amid a deafening roar of musketry. Opdycke emptied his revolver into the Confederates and then used the wooden grip as a club until it shattered.

Colonel Opdycke, shown as a brigadier general
(Library of Congress)

Opdycke's men seized the recessed breastwork, or "retrenchment," that covered the Columbia Pike opening in the main line, and Reilly's reserves surged forward to join them, tipping the balance in the Federals' favor. They managed to drive the Confederates back to the main line, where another close-quarters fight erupted. Among the defenders were 350 Union soldiers armed with Henry repeating rifles capable of firing two-dozen rounds per minute. Southerners who tried to fall back were shot down in a devastating crossfire, while other soldiers in gray hunkered down in the ditch on the front side of the works and continued firing through embrasures in the parapet.

On the Confederate right, the three divisions of Stewart's corps discovered that their front narrowed considerably due to a bend in the Harpeth River, slowing their advance on Reilly's works as brigades crowded together or found their path blocked by other units. Stewart's attack lost cohesion as Southern soldiers struggled through the Osage orange hedges, and then disintegrated as blasts of Union musketry and cannon fire mowed them down. Confederates in Maj. Gen. William W. Loring's division attempted to slip around Reilly's left flank using the Tennessee and Alabama Central Railroad cut, but the guns at Fort Granger swept the cut with shell and case shot, driving them back.

As the leftmost infantry unit in Hood's strike force, Bate's division had the most ground to cover, and it was dusk when his three brigades finally struck Ruger's position. The Confederates penetrated one section of the line occupied by a green Ohio regiment, but veteran Union infantry and artillery quickly sealed the breach. On the far left, Brig. Gen. James R. Chalmers' division of Forrest's cavalry fought dismounted, advancing to within sixty yards of Kimball's line before heavy casualties induced Chalmers to withdraw to a safer distance. From there, the Confederates traded fire with the Federals. On the extreme right, Forrest led Brig. Gen. William H. Jackson's cavalry division across the Harpeth River in an attempt to cut off Schofield's retreat. The dismounted Confederate troopers collided with Wilson's Union cavalry a few miles east of Franklin. Jackson's lead brigade routed a Federal skirmish line, but was then halted by Brig. Gen. Edward Hatch's division—also fighting dismounted—and then driven back across the river.

The final assault of the day occurred after nightfall. Maj. Gen. Edward "Allegheny" Johnson's division of Lee's corps marched blindly in the darkness, the line of battle guided by men carrying flaming torches. As the Confederates approached Ruger's line, they stumbled over the bodies of fallen comrades but remained determined to overrun the Federal position. Three of Johnson's four brigades managed to reach the Union earthworks, only to be pulverized by close-range blasts of musketry and canister. With the repulse of Johnson's assault, the firing gradually diminished and ceased altogether by 2230. After five hours of fighting, the Confederates had failed to carry the Union line at Franklin.

The consequences of Hood's assault at Franklin were devastating to the Army of Tennessee. The Confederates had suffered 6,252 casualties—almost 25 percent of their total strength. But the official tally does not include the 2,000 wounded soldiers who returned to duty shortly after the battle, nor does it reflect the terrible toll on the Army of Tennessee's leadership. The losses included more than 800 commissioned officers, including 13 generals and over 50 regimental commanders. Among the fatalities was General Cleburne, the army's finest combat leader. In attempting to cure the Army of Tennessee of its "frontal assault phobia," Hood had crippled it. But in a message to Richmond, he described the battle as a Confederate victory. The army, he wrote, had "attacked the enemy at Franklin" and had driven them "into their inner lines, which they evacuated during the night, leaving their dead and wounded in our possession, and retired to Nashville, closely pursued by our cavalry. We captured several stand of colors and about 1,000 prisoners." Only in passing did Hood mention "a loss of many gallant officers and brave men."

Fighting on the defensive, the Federals had sustained far fewer casualties than the attacking Confederates: 2,613 killed, wounded, or missing. Over half the losses occurred in the rout of Wagner's division, a disaster that had jeopardized Schofield's entire force and effectively ended Wagner's Army career.

Receiving orders from Thomas to withdraw, Schofield had sent his wagon train across the Harpeth before the battle and resumed the march that night. Although Cox urged him to reconsider in light of the severe drubbing they had given the Confederates, Schofield was anxious to reach the sanctuary of Nashville just twenty miles to the north. The withdrawal began at midnight on 1 December, and by noon, the first of Schofield's troops staggered into Nashville—exhausted from fighting and marching on little food and sleep, yet proudly displaying their captured flags and other trophies of war.

Fortress Rosecrans and Nashville

Hood pursued Schofield to the outskirts of Nashville, and on 2 December, deployed his battered army along a four-mile front, placing Cheatham's corps on the right, Lee's corps—by far the army's largest—in the center, and Stewart's corps on the left. Whittled down to just twenty-one thousand infantry and artillery, the Army of Tennessee was simply too small to cover the flanks, leaving a four-mile gap to the Cumberland River on the left and a one-mile gap on the right. And while the Confederates were near enough to Nashville to glimpse the magnificent Tennessee state capitol, they could also view the Federals' formidable line of earthworks.

Occupied by Union forces since February 1862, Nashville was one of the most heavily fortified cities in the South, protected by an elaborate system of entrenchments that included seven forts and redoubts. Thomas was not satisfied with their location, however, and he immediately put the weary victors of Franklin to work on an expanded outer ring of defenses one mile beyond the inner ring. Exploiting a series of steep ridges, the soldiers constructed an eight-mile semicircular fortification that shielded the southern approaches to Nashville. The flanks were anchored on the Cumberland River, which in turn protected the city's north side, the natural moat augmented by a flotilla of two iron-clads and six gunboats under the command of Lt. Cdr. LeRoy Fitch. Thomas also had managed to scrape together about fifty thousand soldiers at Nashville, including "Smith's Guerrillas," as the rugged veterans of the XVI Corps liked to style themselves. "We are strongly fortified," boasted one Federal soldier, "and all the Rebel hordes could not take the city by assault."

Hood studied Nashville's defenses and came to the same conclusion. Lacking the forces to carry the "Rock City" by assault, he would instead attack the Federal garrison at Murfreesboro, Tennessee, thirty miles to the southeast and force Thomas to march to its relief. Hood had convinced himself that he could crush Thomas in an open-field fight, leaving Sherman no choice but to abandon his campaign in Georgia to rescue "Old Pap," as his soldiers called Thomas. Provoking Thomas into attacking with a superior force was a desperate gamble, but Hood had few options left. He designated Forrest to lead the Murfreesboro expedition. With a force consisting of Buford's and Jackson's cavalry divisions and Bate's infantry division, Forrest was to surround the garrison and prevent it from being reinforced or resupplied.

On 2 December, Bate had set out under orders from Hood to destroy blockhouses, track, and bridges on the Nashville and

Chattanooga Railroad, starting near Murfreesboro and working his way back toward Nashville. Two days later, he attacked a blockhouse about ten miles northwest of Murfreesboro, but withdrew after skirmishing with Union infantry and artillery under Maj. Gen. Robert H. Milroy. Moving on, Bate destroyed three abandoned blockhouses and the bridges they once guarded, and some track. Forrest, meanwhile, pushed out from Nashville, capturing five blockhouses and one troop train—the passengers barely escaping—along the way. On 5 December, the two Confederate forces combined, and Forrest directed that they assault Fortress Rosecrans on the Wilkinson Pike, about half a mile northwest of Murfreesboro. Built in 1863 following the Battle of Stones River, the 225-acre fortified depot bristled with artillery and boasted an 8,000-man garrison commanded by Maj. Gen. Lovell H. Rousseau.

Bate thought storming the fortress suicidal, and he urged Forrest to reconsider. A personal reconnaissance convinced Forrest that Bate was right. On 6 December, Forrest deployed his 6,000-man force—including a recent reinforcement of two small infantry brigades—around Fortress Rosecrans in order to cut off Rousseau's supplies and force the Federals to fight. The next day, Rousseau sent out Milroy on a reconnaissance in force to determine the enemy's location among the cedar trees. In positioning his command between the Confederates and the fortress, Milroy had succeeded in moving his three thousand troops—barely one-half of Forrest's command—beyond Bate's left flank. The Federals advanced to within a few hundred yards of Bate's line, fired several volleys, and then routed the Confederates in a spontaneous charge.

The attack occurred just as the men of Brig. Gen. Jesse J. Finley's Florida brigade received a volley of friendly fire from a Confederate brigade that mistook the Floridians—many of them wearing blue jackets and coats taken at Franklin—for Federals. Forrest and Bate tried to rally the fleeing Southerners, "but they could not be moved by any entreaty or appeal to their patriotism," a disgusted Forrest later reported. Fortunately for the Confederates, while Bate's men fled, Brig. Gen. Abraham Buford's cavalry division dashed into Murfreesboro, inducing Milroy to break off pursuit in order to drive the Southern horsemen from the town. The action of 7 December marked the end of Confederate operations against Fortress Rosecrans, subsequently called the Third Battle of Murfreesboro, the Battle of Wilkinson Pike, or the Battle of the Cedars. The Federals sustained 225 casualties, while the Confederates lost 197 killed, wounded, or missing.

Forrest continued to operate along the railroad between Nashville and Murfreesboro, but he had fewer men to devote to the mission. On 8 December, Hood recalled Bate to Nashville, and in an unequal exchange, sent Forrest an infantry brigade under Col. Charles H. Olmstead. At Hood's behest, Forrest placed part of his cavalry on picket duty along the Cumberland River to detect Union flanking maneuvers. Forrest's infantry wrecked railroad track near Murfreesboro and captured a train carrying soldiers of the 61st Illinois Infantry as well as sixty thousand rations.

Hood, meanwhile, maintained his position south of Nashville and waited for Thomas to move, but Thomas appeared to be in no hurry. On the evening of 1 December, he had informed the Army chief of staff, Maj. Gen. Henry W. Halleck, of his intention to remain inside "the fortifications around Nashville until General Wilson can get his cavalry equipped." Thomas little realized that his reason for delay was political dynamite. Halleck passed his telegram up the chain to Secretary of War Edwin M. Stanton, who showed the message to President Lincoln. "This looks like the McClellan and Rosecrans strategy of do nothing and let the Rebels raid the country," Lincoln fumed, recalling the habitual inaction of Maj. Gen. George. B. McClellan, Maj. Gen. William S. Rosecrans, and certain other Union generals during the first three years of the war.

The president handed the telegram back to Stanton and recommended that General Grant be brought in to prod Thomas into action. On 2 December, Grant fired off two messages urging Thomas to attack Hood at once, but Thomas insisted that his cavalry was numerically inferior to the enemy's, unaware that Forrest's cavalry totaled fewer than six thousand men and that Hood had sent most of his mounted force on an expedition to Murfreesboro. Additional prodding bore little results, with Secretary of War Stanton commenting that if Thomas waited for his cavalry to be ready, "Gabriel will be blowing his last horn."

As the telegraph wires sizzled with urgent messages from Washington, D.C., the weather in middle Tennessee took a sudden wintry turn. On 7 December, a rainstorm closely followed by a blast of arctic air resulted in freezing temperatures and a sheet of ice covering the ground. Thomas decided to wait for better conditions before attacking. Two days later, he yielded to Grant's entreaties and ordered an offensive for 10 December. That afternoon, another winter storm hit, dumping still more sleet and snow, and Thomas reluctantly postponed the assault pending the return of clear weather. At that point, Grant decided to relieve Thomas and had the necessary orders drawn up. But a message from Thomas explaining the reason for the delay convinced Grant to give the "Rock of Chickamauga" one more chance. On 11 December, he ordered Thomas to attack immediately regardless of foul weather or lack of cavalry. Thomas tried to comply, but on the morning of 12 December, the footing on the icy roads and bridges proved so treacherous for the horses that he canceled the offensive. Disgusted, Grant was on the verge of traveling to Nashville to relieve Thomas when word arrived at 2300 on 15 December that Thomas had attacked Hood's army.

Thursday, the fifteenth, had dawned gray and cloudy in Nashville, but the temperatures were already well above freezing. Most of the snow and ice had melted away the previous day thanks to warmer temperatures, leaving behind a sea of mud and a thick blanket of fog. By 0800, the fog had begun to lift, and the Federals had ventured out beyond their fortifications. According to Thomas' plan, General A. J. Smith's corps would spearhead the attack, with Wilson's cavalry corps riding into position on Smith's right and Brig. Gen. Thomas J. Wood's IV Corps forming on Smith's left. Schofield's XXIII Corps would follow in reserve behind Smith. "Smith's Guerrillas" would strike Hood's left flank, while the Federal cavalry swept around it to cut off the Confederates' line of retreat. The IV Corps would support Smith by attacking Hood's center. On the extreme Union left, Maj. Gen. James B. Steedman's division would launch a diversionary attack on Hood's right—held by Cheatham's corps—to prevent the Confederates on that flank from reinforcing the left. Thomas' strike force outnumbered Hood's army by roughly two to one (*Map 7*).

Steedman's command consisted of two brigades of USCTs and a small brigade of white troops. They advanced south along the Murfreesboro Pike under the cover of an artillery barrage, with the black troops leading the way. The Federals wheeled to the right and began to work their way around Cheatham's right flank on Rains Hill, overrunning a thinly held line of rifle pits and dashing into a stand of timber. There they came to a sudden stop. The Nashville and Chattanooga Railroad ran through those woods,

BATTLE OF NASHVILLE
15 December 1864
Initial Confederate Position
Battle Confederate Position
Confederate Movement
Confederate Retreat
Confederate Entrenchments
Initial Union Position
Battle Union Position
Union Attack
Union Movement
Union Entrenchments
0
5000
10000
Feet
Cumberland River
WILSON
SMITH
NASHVILLE
STEEDMAN
STEEDMAN
STEEDMAN
LEBANON PIKE
SCHOFIELD
WOOD
CLEBURNE
MURFREESBORO PIKE
Nashville and Chattanooga RR
SCHOFIELD
SMITH
WOOD
WILSON
Redoubt #1
Redoubt #2
Redoubt #3
Redoubt #4
Redoubt #5
LORING
WALTHALL
GRANNY WHITE PIKE
Montgomery Hill
CHEATHAM
Rains Hill
S. D. LEE
STEWART
FRANKLIN PIKE
Tennessee and Alabama Central RR
HILLSBORO PIKE
Compton Hill
Overton Hill

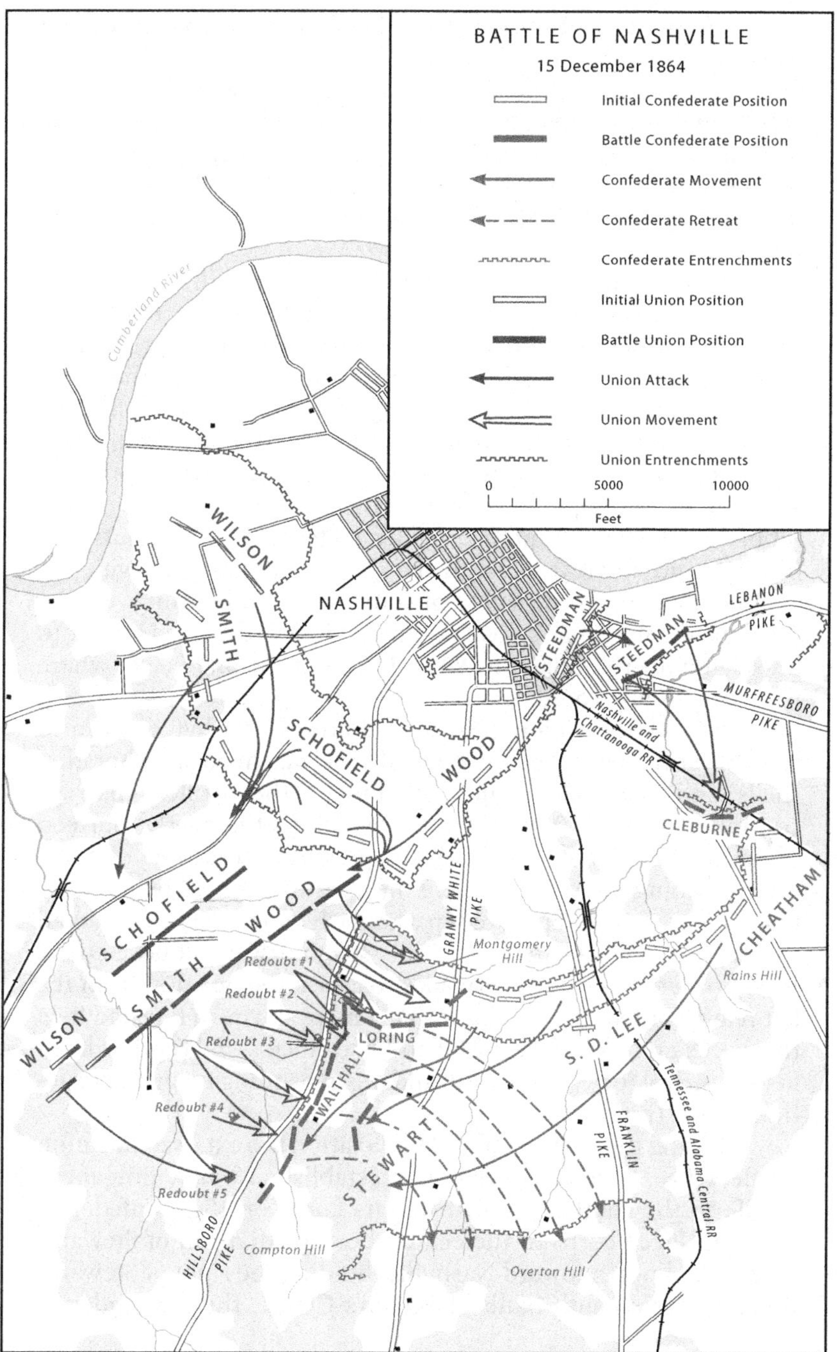

MAP 7

and a twenty-foot-deep cut blasted out of solid rock stretched before them. As the line of Union soldiers halted at the railroad cut, point-blank rounds of musketry and canister blew gaping holes in their ranks. Although one of Steedman's brigade commanders had reconnoitered the enemy's right flank the night before, he did not see the railroad cut within the belt of timber, nor had he realized that the log bastion on the Confederate right flank was a lunette mounting four guns.

The Confederates manning this part of the line were from Cleburne's division, and they were eager to avenge both their late commander and those of their comrades who had fallen at Franklin. Their devastating fire proved too much for the black soldiers, most of whom were seeing combat for the first time. Many jumped into the cut and almost all were shot down, while the rest turned and fled to the rear. Steedman's white brigade, meanwhile, attempted to storm the lunette but was easily repulsed. The three Union brigades re-formed on the outskirts of town and spent the rest of the day exchanging fire with the Confederates from the safety of some brick outbuildings on the Rains farm. Steedman's diversion had failed to deceive Hood into bolstering his right flank by stripping troops from his left, where the main attack would occur.

At 1000, the Union guns in and around Nashville began to roar. Soon the air above the enemy's line was filled with bursting shells and billowing clouds of smoke. The artillery barrage continued until 1230. As the guns fell silent, the nearly fourteen thousand soldiers of Wood's IV Corps advanced in line of battle toward Montgomery Hill, where the earthworks held by Stewart's Confederate corps appeared particularly formidable. To avoid making a frontal assault up the hill's steep forward slope, General Wood ordered one of his brigades to attack the position from the left rear. Word soon came back that a mere skirmish line had held the works on Montgomery Hill and had since fled. Wood ordered his command to occupy the hill and dig in pending further instructions from Thomas.

Finding the Montgomery Hill position too exposed to Union artillery fire, General Stewart had established a new line about a mile to the south. Like Cheatham's corps on the Confederate right and Lee's corps in the center, Loring's division of Stewart's corps faced north toward Nashville, holding the right of Stewart's line along the south bank of Brown's Creek. The remainder of

Stewart's corps was drawn up along the Hillsboro Pike, facing west. The men had not had time to entrench. Instead, Hood relied on a series of five mutually supporting redoubts—each one defended by several guns and a few companies from Maj. Gen. Edward C. Walthall's division—and a double stone wall that bordered either side of the road to provide sufficient protection for his refused left flank.

On the Union right, the twenty thousand soldiers of Wilson's and Smith's corps executed a gigantic left wheel and then bore down on Stewart's line along the Hillsboro Pike. Advancing on the outside of the Federals' massive swinging arc, Wilson's dismounted troopers had to double-quick to keep pace with Smith's infantry, who had far less ground to cover. The Union cavalrymen routed the Confederates of Brig. Gen. Mathew D. Ector's infantry brigade under Col. David Coleman and captured General Chalmers' headquarters wagons, which the Southern cavalry commander had entrusted to the foot soldiers' care. The Federals next attacked Redoubt No. 5, Stewart's leftmost bastion. Brig. Gen. Edward Hatch's cavalry division struck first, closely followed by Brig. Gen. John McArthur's infantry division. The 1,500 Northern attackers soon overwhelmed the 150 Confederate defenders, but their victory celebration was cut short by a heavy fire of musketry and canister from Redoubt No. 4, commanded by Capt. Charles Lumsden. Catching their breath, Hatch's and McArthur's men stormed Lumsden's redoubt and captured it after a brief hand-to-hand struggle.

While Hatch's cavalry and McArthur's first and second infantry brigades attacked Redoubt No. 4, the commander of McArthur's third brigade, Col. Sylvester G. Hill, noted that Redoubt No. 3 was directing its fire on the Union strike force. Hill was eager to storm the third enemy fort, but General Smith told him to wait until another brigade could be brought up to support him. No sooner did Smith ride off to find the brigade than Hill ordered his bugler to sound the charge. The men dashed forward, yelling at the top of their lungs. Much to the attackers' relief, the Confederates fired over their heads, causing few casualties. By the time the Federals had clambered into the fort, most of the Confederates were gone, leaving behind two guns. Hill then called on his men to storm Redoubt No. 2. Moments later, a Confederate minié ball struck Hill in the head, killing him instantly. His second in command, Col. William R. Marshall, led two hundred men against the second fort and drove off the defenders, who in their haste abandoned one cannon, one caisson, and a large amount of equipment.

With the capture of redoubts two through five, the Federals were threatening to roll up Stewart's entire refused line. Hood had ordered S. D. Lee to send reinforcements to strengthen Stewart's left flank, and Lee dispatched two brigades from Johnson's division. They arrived too late to save any of the redoubts and merely huddled behind the stone wall along the eastern side of the Hillsboro Pike. When Union artillery opened fire on them, many of Johnson's men panicked and fled to the rear. Others remained cowering behind the stone wall and were fired on by McArthur's skirmishers, who had advanced to the wall on the western side of the road. The Federals then launched a bayonet charge and captured about 450 prisoners from Johnson's division. To bolster Stewart's crumbling flank, General Walthall pulled one of his brigades from the right of his line and sent it racing to the left.

During the advance of the Union right, Smith's infantry had diverged from Wilson's cavalry, leaving a sizable gap in the Federal line. Thomas directed Schofield to bring up the XXIII Corps and deploy it on the right of Smith's corps. Soon afterward, a brigade of the XXIII Corps and a brigade of Wilson's cavalry swept around Stewart's left flank and drove into the rear of the Confederate position. The Federals collided with a battery that Stewart had shifted from Loring's front as well as the remnant of Johnson's two brigades. Firing a few ragged volleys at the oncoming blue line, Johnson's men once again sprinted away, abandoning three cannons to the enemy. Some grateful Union cavalrymen wheeled the guns around and opened fire on the fleeing Confederates.

Realizing that his refused line was rapidly disintegrating, Stewart ordered his entire corps to retreat, but Walthall's hard-pressed division was already falling back. Wood's Union IV Corps, meanwhile, lurched into action and assaulted Loring's position. Most of Loring's troops had already withdrawn from their earth-works, but the artillery crews in Redoubt No. 1 continued to fight until the Federals had overrun the fort. The attackers captured three guns and forty prisoners. Stewart's corps was now in full flight down the Granny White Pike—only nightfall had saved it from destruction. At 1500, Hood had told Cheatham to rein-force Stewart's left flank, but the two divisions did not get under way until that evening. In the meantime, the brigade holding the extreme left of Lee's position formed a line facing west to guard against a flank attack.

Hood witnessed the stampede of Stewart's corps from a hilltop near the Granny White Pike. Despite the rout, he was willing to risk all on another defensive stand, mindful that a defeat would probably cost him his command. He deployed his army along a chain of hills a few miles south of the previous line. Hood's new line was far more compact than its predecessor, stretching roughly three miles from Compton Hill near the Granny White Pike eastward to Overton Hill on the Franklin Pike. Cheatham's corps anchored the left, Stewart's corps occupied the center, and Lee's corps held the right. Hood's army was heavily outnumbered, and only Lee's corps remained relatively unscathed by the recent battles. Worse yet, Forrest and most of his mounted troops were still at Murfreesboro, leaving Hood with only Chalmers' cavalry division to guard his flanks against Wilson's Union cavalry corps.

Thomas, meanwhile, informed Washington of his success, reporting the capture of seventeen guns and fifteen hundred prisoners. Grant congratulated Thomas on his "splendid victory" and urged him to give the enemy "no rest until he is utterly destroyed." Thomas had every intention of completing the work begun on 15 December. On the following morning, his forces were aligned as they had been the previous day, with Steedman on the Union left, Wood and Smith holding the center, and Schofield and Wilson occupying the right. The day was warm and spring-like, and by 0830, the sun had burned off most of the early morning fog. The Federals cautiously advanced to within six hundred yards of the Confederate line and then halted. Fearing an attack, Schofield appealed to Thomas and Smith for reinforcements, even though Thomas had already sent him an entire division from Smith's corps. An exasperated General Smith refused to send a second division to Schofield because it would leave him with just one division, and Schofield refused to attack until he was reinforced.

Schofield's apprehension stemmed from a dispatch that Wilson had sent both him and Thomas, reporting that a heavy column of Confederate infantry was moving west for an apparent assault on the Union right flank. Wilson also indicated that the ground in his front was unsuitable for cavalry operations. Thomas rode out to Wilson's headquarters to spur his cavalry commander into action. But Wilson expressed his concerns regarding the enemy's intentions and once more suggested that his cavalry be shifted to the left flank. Growing impatient, Thomas refused to consider Wilson's suggestion and instead ordered him to develop Hood's intentions by advancing toward the Granny White Pike. Once Wilson had reached the pike, Thomas explained, the rest of the army could launch the assault. Thomas then rode off to other parts of the Union line to determine their readiness to attack. In the meantime, morning dragged into afternoon, and sunshine gave way to gray skies and a light rain that soon developed into a downpour.

After a lengthy delay, the Union assault began around midafternoon on 16 December, and it unfolded much as the attack of the previous day had. Once again, Thomas launched a diversionary assault on the Confederate right to deceive Hood into shifting troops from his left, where the main attack would occur. First, Union artillery pounded the Confederate position on Overton Hill, which was held by Maj. Gen. Henry D. Clayton's division of Lee's corps. Then Steedman's two USCT brigades and two brigades of Brig. Gen. Samuel Beatty's IV Corps division attacked Clayton's line, advancing into a storm of canister and minié balls that claimed over a thousand casualties, including one of Beatty's brigade commanders, Col. Philip S. Post, who suffered a grievous hip wound but survived and later became a U.S. congressman and diplomat. The USCTs' line of battle swept across a cornfield and diverged when it came to an overgrown thicket. The line began to fragment as the men climbed over a rail fence and worked their way through a series of felled trees; then the line dissolved as the soldiers became ensnared in the tangled branches of the abatis or hugged the ground on the forward slope of Overton Hill. On Steedman's right, Beatty's assault also failed to penetrate the Confederate line (*Map 8*).

At this point, the 13th USCT raced up the slope past their prone comrades and headed straight for the enemy's works. Clayton's troops concentrated all their firepower on the 13th USCT, whose color-bearer brought the regimental flag to the Confederate parapet before he was shot down. Five more soldiers seized the colors and met the same fate. Within minutes, the regiment lost 220 officers and men, roughly 40 percent of its strength. Brig. Gen. James T. Holtzclaw, the Confederate commander in that sector, paid tribute to the valor of the 13th USCT in his after action report. "I have seen most of the battle-fields of the West," he wrote, "but never saw dead men thicker than in front of my

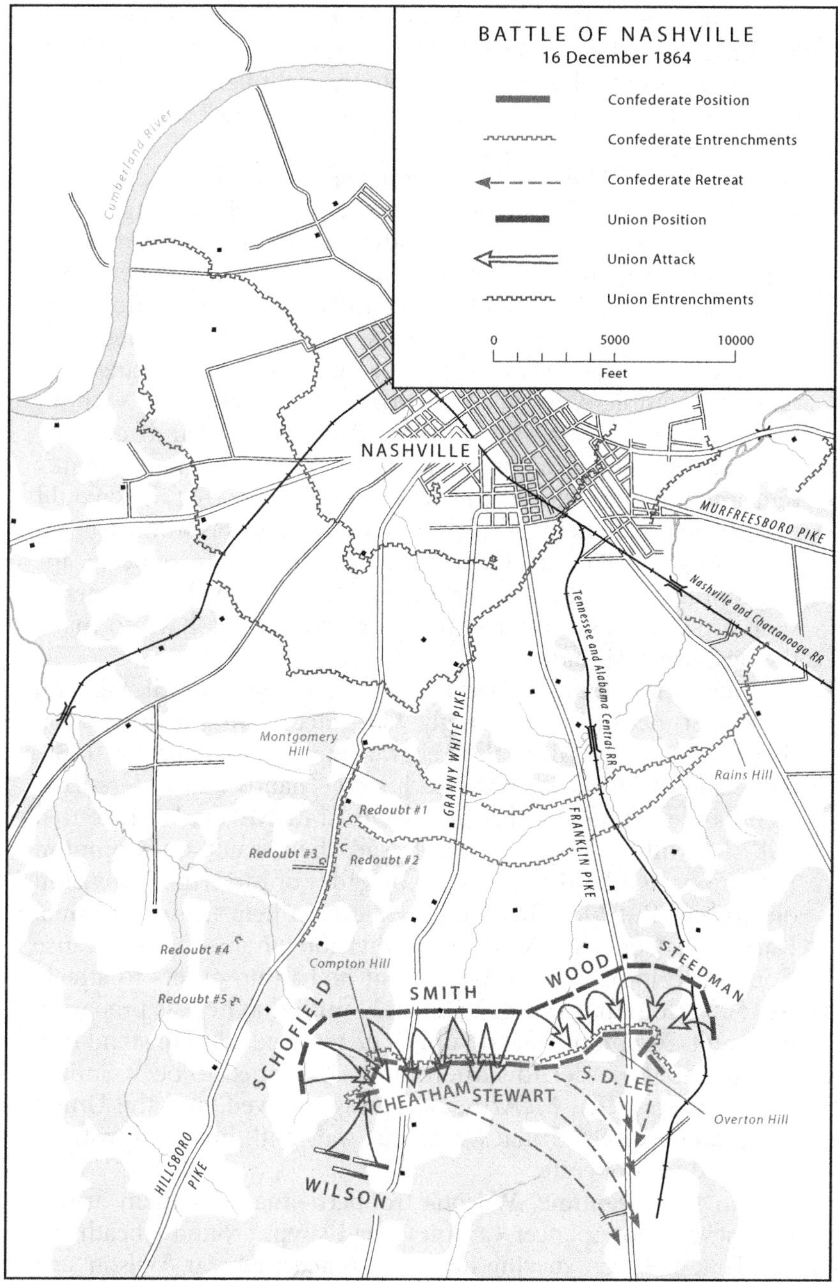

BATTLE OF NASHVILLE
16 December 1864
Confederate Position
Confederate Entrenchments
Confederate Retreat
Union Position
Union Attack
Union Entrenchments
0
5000
10000
Feet
Cumberland River
NASHVILLE
MURFREESBORO PIKE
Nashville and Chattanooga RR
Tennessee and Alabama Central RR
Montgomery Hill
Rains Hill
GRANNY WHITE PIKE
FRANKLIN PIKE
Redoubt #1
Redoubt #3
Redoubt #2
Redoubt #4
Compton Hill
STEEDMAN
WOOD
Redoubt #5
SCHOFIELD
SMITH
S. D. LEE
CHEATHAM
STEWART
Overton Hill
HILLSBORO PIKE
WILSON

two right regiments." This time, however, Steedman's diversionary assault achieved its objective: Hood ordered Cheatham to rush two brigades of Cleburne's division to the right flank, even though Cheatham had already stretched his own line to the breaking point in order to cover his overextended left flank.

The key to Cheatham's position was Compton Hill. It dominated the surrounding countryside, its steep slopes suggesting that a frontal assault would be bloody work. Despite its formidable appearance, the hill possessed some serious flaws as a defensive stronghold. First, it was vulnerable to Union artillery fire on its northern and western faces. Second, the hill was crowned with a line of entrenchments that the exhausted Confederates had failed to complete, leaving the works too shallow and without head logs and abatis. But their third and worst handicap only became apparent at daybreak. In the darkness, the men of Bate's division had dug their earthworks in such a way that they would not have a clear field of fire until the enemy was almost upon them. General Bate decided that it was too late to relocate, for the continual musketry and artillery fire along the line rendered such a move foolhardy. His troops would simply have to make the best of the situation.

Just a few hundred yards north of Compton Hill, General McArthur became increasingly frustrated with the indecision that seemed to paralyze the Federal senior leadership. By 1430, he decided to take matters into his own hands and ordered the commander of his first brigade, Colonel McMillen, "to take that hill." McMillen's brigade would lead the assault on Compton Hill, supported by the other two brigades of McArthur's division on his left. But McMillen could expect no help from Maj. Gen. Darius N. Couch's XXIII Corps division on his right because Couch had informed McArthur that he had no orders to attack. At 1500, McArthur notified General Smith that he was preparing to assault Compton Hill, and unless he received word to stand fast, would give the order to start. Thomas happened to be at Smith's headquarters when McArthur's message arrived, and the Union commander directed that McArthur wait until he could instruct Schofield to cooperate.

In the meantime, Wilson's troopers—many of them armed with seven-shot Spencer carbines—had swept around Cheatham's left flank and were driving into the Confederate rear. Wilson sent several messages to Schofield urging him to advance but received no answer. He therefore sped over to Schofield's headquarters, where he found Thomas trying to prod a reluctant Schofield into attacking Compton Hill. Wilson informed the two generals that his cavalry was driving the enemy and would soon cut off his line of retreat. Just then Thomas lifted his field glasses and observed McMillen's brigade swarming up Compton Hill. He calmly turned to Schofield and said, "General, will you please advance your whole line."

Thomas' dispatch to McArthur had arrived too late to stop McMillen, who attacked at 1600 as ordered. His Midwesterners clambered up the steep northwestern slope of the hill, some of them coming under "a perfect storm of musket balls," noted one Federal soldier. But most of McMillen's men were surprised at the absence of musketry along their front until they came to the smoke-shrouded crest of the hill and suddenly found themselves within point-blank range of Bate's works. McMillen recalled that the defenders fired a nervous volley that sailed over their heads. The Federals then gave a yell and jumped over the parapet. The fighting was at close quarters with fixed bayonets and clubbed muskets. During the melee, Lt. Col. Samuel P. Jennison of the 10th Minnesota Infantry fell mortally wounded, while a few yards away, Lt. Col. William M. Shy, the commander of a Tennessee infantry regiment, was killed instantly by a bullet that struck him above the right eye. Afterward the ground he had died defending was renamed Shy's Hill.

General McArthur, shown here as a colonel
(Library of Congress)

With Wilson's cavalry striking from the rear, Schofield's troops attacking on McMillen's right, and McArthur's other two brigades driving forward on the left, Cheatham's entire defensive line soon collapsed under the sheer weight of the Union onslaught. As the Confederate left flank crumbled, the center held by Stewart's corps followed suit. A disorganized mass of panic-stricken Confederates fled south down the Granny White Pike, discarding their weapons and equipment, with Wilson's cavalry in hot pursuit. During the rout, the Southerners abandoned fifty-three guns, nearly one-half of their artillery. Here and there Confederate officers—including General Hood and his staff—tried in vain to stem the rout.

On the right, Lee's corps still held fast, but as Steedman's and Wood's forces converged on Lee's position, the Confederates began to run. Only Clayton's division on Overton Hill remained more or less intact, earning it the unenviable task of serving as the army's rear guard on the Franklin Pike. Chalmers' cavalry division performed a similar service on the Granny White Pike. One of Chalmers' brigade commanders, Col. Edward W. Rucker, was wounded and captured during a desperate struggle with units of Hatch's Union cavalry division. In the end, the combination of darkness, exhaustion, and a driving rainstorm brought the Federal pursuit to a halt, saving the Army of Tennessee from probable destruction.

In Nashville, Union Army and civilian hospitals as well as numerous homes, churches, and public buildings were filled with thousands of wounded and dying men from both Thomas' and Hood's armies. The two-day battle had cost the Federals 3,061 casualties, while the Confederate losses are uncertain, given the paucity of data supplied by the army's medical director and unit commanders. General Thomas reported capturing 4,462 prisoners, and historian Wiley Sword estimates that the Confederates lost about 2,300 killed and wounded, for a total loss of 6,800. In just under three weeks—from the skirmish at Spring Hill to the second day at Nashville—the Army of Tennessee had suffered nearly 14,000 combat casualties, more than one-third of the men Hood had led into Tennessee.

On the morning of 17 December, Wilson's cavalry resumed the pursuit, with Wood's IV Corps infantry following close behind. The Federal horsemen struck Lee's rear guard about four miles north of Franklin and routed it in a mounted saber charge. The Confederates made another stand at the Harpeth River and yet again five miles south of Franklin, while the main body continued to Spring Hill. Commanding the rear guard, Lee was wounded in the foot by a shell fragment. The Union infantry was delayed at the crossing of the Harpeth while engineers rebuilt the trestle bridge.

On the evening of 18 December, Forrest rejoined the Army of Tennessee at Columbia, having received word from Hood of the disaster at Nashville. The next day, he opposed the Federal cavalry's crossing of Rutherford's Creek—which had flooded its banks—while the Confederates crossed the Duck River a few miles to the south. At 1500, he withdrew to Columbia, where Hood placed him in command of the army's rear guard and augmented his cavalry with nineteen hundred infantry under General Walthall. On 20 December, while the Confederate main body made its way toward Pulaski, Forrest contested Wilson's crossing of the Duck River. In the meantime, the Federals' pontoon train arrived at last. The Union army used a pontoon bridge to cross Rutherford's Creek on 21 December and the Duck River over the next two days.

The Army of Tennessee, meanwhile, passed through Pulaski and by 24 December had marched to within ten miles of the Tennessee River. Brig. Gen. John T. Croxton's Federal cavalry brigade skirmished with Forrest's rear guard for much of the day. During the fight at Richland Creek, one of Forrest's division commanders, General Buford, was wounded, and a Union trooper captured Chalmers' headquarters flag.

On Christmas Day, the Confederates reached the Tennessee River near Bainbridge, Alabama, and laid their pontoon bridge. In the meantime, Col. Thomas J. Harrison's brigade of Wilson's cavalry corps groped through thick woods and collided with Forrest's rear guard, which was drawn up behind a rail barricade at the top of Anthony's Hill. The Confederates fired a point-blank volley into the Federals' faces, and then Forrest ordered a charge. Eager for revenge, the Southerners routed Harrison's troopers, capturing one Union gun and inflicting about 150 casualties. The next morning, as the Army of Tennessee began to cross the river several miles to the south, Col. John H. Hammond's Union cavalry brigade waded across Sugar Creek amid a dense fog and blundered into another ambush. Once again, Forrest's men fired a devastating volley and then launched a counterattack, chasing the terrified Federals across the creek. The skirmish at Sugar Creek marked the final engagement between the armies of Thomas and Hood.

The Army of Tennessee completed its crossing of the Tennessee River on 27 December. With the Confederates safely across and the Federals running low on supplies, Thomas abandoned the pursuit. But as the main column returned to Nashville, a Union cavalry force under Col. William J. Palmer set out from Decatur, Alabama, toward Hood's army and managed to destroy its pontoon train as well as a large supply train. Worse yet, other supplies bound for the army failed to arrive because of a break in the Mobile and Ohio Railroad. The Confederates nevertheless reached their destination at Tupelo by 12 January 1865 and went into winter camp.

At the start of the campaign, the Army of Tennessee had numbered about 38,000, exclusive of Forrest's cavalry. As of 20 January 1865, the army was down to 18,708 present for duty—a loss of more than one-half of its strength. According to General Beauregard, however, the number of men who were actually present was closer to 15,000. Fewer still were fit for duty. Many lacked shoes and adequate clothing, nearly all were underfed, and discipline was virtually nonexistent. In the words of Beauregard's inspector general, Col. Alfred Roman, "If not in the strict sense of the word, a disorganized mob, it was no longer an army." His dreams of glory shattered, Hood submitted his resignation to President Davis, and Davis accepted it on 23 January 1865. Soon afterward, remnants of the Army of Tennessee were sent to Mobile and North Carolina in what would be the Confederate army's last major troop transfer.

Like his adversary Hood, Thomas had fought his last battle. And like the Army of Tennessee, a large part of his command would

---

A detail from Grant and his Generals, *by Ole P. H. Balling, depicting (l. to r.)*
Sheridan, Thomas, Meade, Sherman, and Grant
(Library of Congress)

soon be sent elsewhere—Schofield's XXIII Corps to eastern North Carolina and Wilson's cavalry corps to Alabama and Georgia. But the Battle of Nashville had enhanced Thomas' reputation just as surely as it had destroyed Hood's. He had gained entry into the pantheon of generals who ranked foremost in saving the Union: Ulysses S. Grant, William T. Sherman, Philip H. Sheridan, George G. Meade, and George H. Thomas.

Analysis

The Battles of Franklin and Nashville wrecked the Confederacy's second-largest field army, crushing the hopes of soldiers and civilians in Mississippi, Tennessee, and elsewhere in the Confederacy. "All was confusion and disarray," lamented one Army of Tennessee veteran who endured both the carnage at Franklin and the collapse at Nashville. The two battles convinced him that "the Confederacy was indeed gone up, and that we were a ruined people."

While Thomas pursued Hood south of Nashville, Confederate morale suffered another severe blow in Georgia. On 21 December, Sherman captured Savannah and presented the city to President Lincoln as a Christmas gift. The success of the campaigns in Georgia and Tennessee fully justified the risk that Sherman had taken in sending part of his army northward with Thomas to deal with Forrest and Hood, while he led the remainder on a raid deep into hostile territory. The risk as Sherman understood it was minimal, for he had already accomplished a similar feat—albeit on a smaller scale—in the Meridian Campaign. Sherman also knew that his superiority in manpower and materiel enabled him to conduct two campaigns at once, and he trusted Thomas to defeat Hood. "Old Pap" did not disappoint him.

Despite continual pressure from Grant, Thomas had refused to launch an attack at Nashville until he deemed his forces ready and the conditions right. He had staked his Army career on this decision and had come within a whisker of being removed. But his strength of character had prevailed during the difficult time just prior to the Battle of Nashville, enabling him to achieve one of the war's few decisive victories.

Thomas was also fortunate in having subordinates whose skill as combat commanders more than compensated for Schofield's deficiencies. At Franklin, Schofield wisely designated General Cox as commander of the Union defensive line south of town, and Cox acquitted himself superbly, with ample assistance from lower-ranking officers such as Reilly, Ruger, and Opdycke. At Nashville, however, Cox was superseded by the far less able General Couch. Deprived of his right-hand man, Schofield took counsel of his fears and refused to attack on the sixteenth of December. Fortunately for Thomas, two other subordinates, Wilson and McArthur, seized the initiative and attacked anyway, much as Thomas' troops had done at Missionary Ridge the previous year.

Of all the blunders that Hood committed during the Tennessee Campaign, the first—and perhaps foremost—was the decision to wait two weeks at Tuscumbia while his commissary officers collected provisions and Forrest raided Johnsonville. This interval gave Thomas invaluable time to concentrate his forces at Nashville and virtually ensured that Hood would have to fight a numerically superior foe. After the bloodbath at Franklin, Hood's options became severely limited, but he did not have to confront Thomas' force at Nashville, as has often been argued. Instead, he could have attacked Fortress Rosecrans with his entire army rather than an undersized expeditionary force. The losses might have been heavy, but the windfall of supplies would have benefited his army greatly, and such a demonstration might have induced Thomas to attack before he was ready, which had been the main object of the Forrest expedition.

Throughout 1864, Forrest had demonstrated the difference that one great leader can make in warfare—and yet his successes were never enough to tip the balance in the Confederacy's favor. Even so, his achievements were impressive. He had routed superior forces under W. S. Smith and Sturgis, forcing Sherman to send one of his best corps commanders after him. Although Forrest had suffered defeat at Tupelo, he had prevented fourteen thousand veteran troops from joining Sherman's army group during the Atlanta Campaign. But Forrest never succeeded in cutting Sherman's supply line, and even his Johnsonville raid had scarcely put a dent in the Union army's logistical apparatus. If his service during the Tennessee Campaign lacked the brilliance of his independent raids, it nevertheless revealed Forrest's ability to function in a more conventional role, screening Hood's army and serving as its eyes and ears. Above all, Forrest's handling of the army's rear guard during the retreat from Nashville was a testament to the endurance and fighting spirit of his troops and to the indomitable will of their commander.

Unfortunately for the Confederacy, Hood had squandered its most precious military asset—its manpower—and no amount of fighting spirit could compensate for that loss. As the fighting at Nashville had demonstrated, the Union Army's ranks were filled with thousands of USCTs who were just as willing to die for their freedom as their adversaries were willing to die for their independence. Nor was that all: thousands of Union soldiers wielded Henry and Spencer repeating rifles and carbines, giving them an overwhelming firepower advantage against the Confederates, whose main weapon remained the single-shot rifle musket. Outmanned, outgunned, and outgeneraled, the remnants of the once-mighty Army of Tennessee nevertheless refused to admit defeat. "I doubt if any soldiers in the world ever needed more cumulative evidence to convince them that they were beaten," Schofield wrote. And so the war would grind on into its fifth year.

The Author

Derek W. Frisby is a middle Tennessee native, a U.S. Marine Corps veteran of Operations DESERT SHIELD and DESERT STORM, and a graduate of the University of Alabama, where he earned his doctorate in history. He is an associate professor of Global Studies and Cultural Geography at Middle Tennessee State University, where he teaches courses on Tennessee history, military geography, and global warfare and culture. Professor Frisby also leads staff rides and tours of Tennessee Civil War battlefields, and he conducts courses on warfare and public memory in such diverse places as Iwo Jima, Peleliu, Guam, Europe, and Vietnam.

FURTHER READINGS

Connelly, Donald B. *John M. Schofield and the Politics of Generalship.* Chapel Hill: University of North Carolina Press, 2006.

Cox, Jacob D. *The Battle of Franklin, Tennessee, November 30, 1864: A Monograph.* New York: C. Scribner's Sons, 1897.

———. *The March to the Sea: Franklin and Nashville, Campaigns of the Civil War,* Vol. 10. New York: C. Scribner's Sons, 1882.

Dobak, William A. *Freedom by the Sword: The U.S. Colored Troops, 1862–1867.* Washington, D.C.: U.S. Army Center of Military History, 2011.

Hess, Earl J. *The Civil War in the West: Victory and Defeat from the Appalachians to the Mississippi.* Chapel Hill: University of North Carolina Press, 2012.

Sword, Wiley. *The Confederacy's Last Hurrah: Spring Hill, Franklin, and Nashville.* Lawrence: University Press of Kansas, 1993.

Wills, Brian Steel. *A Battle from the Start: The Life of Nathan Bedford Forrest.* New York: HarperCollins, 1992.

———. *George Henry Thomas: As True as Steel.* Lawrence: University Press of Kansas, 2012.

For more information on the U.S. Army in the Civil War, please read other titles in the U.S. Army Campaigns of the Civil War series published by the U.S. Army Center of Military History. (www.history.army.mil)